NIHONGO DAISUKI!

JAPANESE FOR CHILDREN
THROUGH GAMES AND SONGS

A TEACHER'S MANUAL
complete with photo-ready materials

BY SUSAN H. HIRATE and NORIKO KAWAURA

Bess Press, Inc.
P. O. Box 22388
Honolulu, HI 96822

Illustrations: Kasumi Ochiai and Natalie Kikkawa
Cover: Z. Harris

Copyright ©   1990 by Bess Press, Inc.
ALL RIGHTS RESERVED
Printed in the United States of America
ISBN: 0-935848-82-7

Library of Congress
CATALOG CARD NO.:   89-081822

Hirate, Susan H. and Noriko Kawaura

NIHONGO DAISUKI!
    Japanese for Children Through Games and Songs

Honolulu, Hawaii: Bess Press, Inc.
208 pages   illustration, appendix

TABLE OF CONTENTS

PREFACE

This manual is the result of a TITLE II grant from the U. S. Department of Education Secretary's Discretionary Fund for Mathematics, Science, and Critical Foreign Languages. Our goal was to come up with a proficiency-based curriculum for elementary-age children who were learning spoken Japanese for the first time.

Our first task was to establish the <u>contexts</u> that children identify with, and the functions that they acquire, and organize them into some orderly sequence. We decided that, for the first year, the most natural context would be the classroom. The functions focus on <u>self</u> with respect to what goes on in the classroom.

Given this contextual framework, we then proceeded to devise lesson plans that would both introduce new material and reenforce previously introduced material in a <u>fun</u> way. Grammatical rules are not overtly introduced at all.

Our overall goal is to offer a "taste" of the Japanese language, with the hope that those who like what they "tasted" will come back for more, later on.

We want to make it clear that the emphasis is on aural/oral skills, (listening and speaking); reading and writing are not introduced, thus reprieving us of the troublesome task of dealing with romanization. For children who are still at the stage of learning to spell English words, imagine how visually confusing words like <u>remon</u>, <u>appuru</u>, and <u>raion</u> can be!

The final and perhaps most controversial decision has to do with speech styles. Should we expect children to speak in a formal style or should we expose them to more natural, informal speech that is typical of the speech of native Japanese children? While the latter choice sounds logical, there are pros and cons to both sides. Children should speak like children, but the danger of teaching "natural, children's speech" is that the student may unknowingly continue to use informal speech later in life in situations that demand more formality. This is quite evident in adults who learn "street Japanese" (as opposed to textbook Japanese) -- their speech tends to sound too casual in some situations. The reverse situation, however, does not seem to be as much of a problem. That is, it is easier to learn informal speech after internalizing formal speech, but not vice versa.

On the other hand, if our goal is "natural" Japanese, then "children's speech" is the clear choice. We assume that those who go on to study more Japanese will do so in a systematic way that will introduce them to the various speech styles associated with "growing up." Also, at this very beginning level of Japanese, the students' speaking proficiency will hover at the word/phrase level (not sentences). Therefore, the problem of fossilization is minimal.

Nevetheless, we have decided to give the teacher the option of deciding between formal and informal speech by providing both. Given the varying classroom situations (types of students, their language backgrounds, etc.) we feel that only the teacher himself can make the appropriate final decision. In the vocabulary lists, a word followed by a word in parentheses means that the combined utterance may be considered formal. For example, "good morning" is noted as *ohayoo (gozaimasu)*--*ohayoo* is informal and *ohayoo gozaimasu* is formal.

In summary, the following points should be kept in mind.

1. this curriculum emphasizes aural/oral skills; no reading or writing
2. first-year context is the classroom; second-year context goes beyond the classroom
3. little or no grammar explanations
4. choice between formal/informal speech
5. overall goal is to provide a "taste" of spoken Japanese

We wish to acknowledge the following people for their support and encouragement in realizing this book: Dr. Patricia Steinhoff, Principal Investigator; Dr. Cynthia Ning, Project Director and Investigator; and Dr. David Ashworth, Co-Investigator of the original grant that spawned this book; and Mr. Dale Spaulding, State Resource Teacher for the Elementary Second Language Program, who recommended using the original draft of this book in DOE classrooms. We also wish to thank the graphic artists, Ms. Kasumi Ochiai and especially Ms. Natalie Kikkawa, for their artwork.

In addition, we wish to thank the many teachers who provided us with valuable feedback on the original draft.

Susan H. Hirate
Noriko Kawaura

INTRODUCTION

This is a teacher's manual designed for use in the elementary school classroom. It contains activities and games which introduce basic elements of spoken first-year Japanese, geared for upper-elementary (grades 4-6) students. Most of these activities have been tried in various sixth grade classes with much success.

This manual provides suggested lesson plans for approximately one school year, based on two 30-minute classes a week, for approximately 25 weeks (i.e. one academic year, minus holidays, vacations, etc.)

Each lesson plan contains a suggested vocabulary list, suggested dialogues, games and activities, and copy-ready visuals and materials for the teacher and students. Worksheets to be used as homework assignments are not provided, so such worksheets (if deemed necessary) must be devised by the individual teacher.

When using these materials, we request that the teacher keep the following points in mind:

1. The vocabulary lists are *suggested* lists and should be adjusted according to the user's "domain." e.g. FRUITS: pineapples and papayas might be appropriate for Hawaii, but not so appropriate in New York.

2. The dialogues provided are also *suggested* dialogues which may be adjusted accordingly by the teacher.

3. It is recommended that the teacher use Japanese as much as possible from Day One.

    example: Teacher: Hai, minasan, yoku kiite kudasai.
    (gestures with hands and ears)

Copy-ready visuals for the various games and activities are provided at the back and have been coded to correspond with the appropriate unit. Some materials require more preparation than copying and, in such cases, instructions are included.

example: Unit 3. Tell Me About Your Family
             Day 1

             Materials: fingerdolls (3a)

             (3a) refers to the code number of the particular material required, which is located in the appendix by the same number.

Suggestions for preparing and preserving the copy-ready materials:

1. use color: since all of the visuals are black and white drawings, coloring them appropriately would enhance their usage.

2. protect: laminate the visuals. If that is not possible, insert them into photo album pages to protect them.

3. permanent sets: certain materials (flash cards for students' use, for example) should also be laminated, if possible.

FIRST-YEAR *JAPANESE* FOR ELEMENTARY CHILDREN

UNIT	CONTENT/CONTEXT	FUNCTION
01	**FIRST DAY OF SCHOOL**	
	1. greetings	to handle basic courtesy expressions
	2. courtesy expressions	in social interactions
	3. roll call	
02	**TELL ME ABOUT YOURSELF**	
	1. self-introductions	to state one's own name
	2. identifying others by name	to handle common personal names
	3. talking about self	to ask and answer by name
	4. asking about others	to state one's age and grade
		to state one's telephone number, address
		to ask about someone else's telephone number and address
03	**TELL ME ABOUT YOUR FAMILY**	
	1. family terms	to identify family terms
	2. counters: ages, number of people	to state names of one's family members
	3. occupations	to provide and ask ages of family members
		to provide and ask information concerning professions of one's family members
04	**DO WHAT THE TEACHER SAYS**	
	1. classroom instructions	to recognize simple daily activities
	2. basic verbs in daily life	to follow simple instructions
	3. following instructions	to recognize commands and follow
	4. giving instructions	
05	**MY FAVORITE FOODS**	
	1. names of fruits and vegetables	to recognize names of fruits and vegetables
	2. colors	to specify color, shape, taste, and size of fruits and vegetables
	3. description: textures, shapes, tastes	to state preferences
	4. likes/dislikes	

06   GOING TO THE STORE

1. numbers	to recognize 1 - 100
2. money	to count from 1 - 100
3. counting	to recognize names of shops
4. objects/colors/descriptions	to recognize items of clothing
5. names of shops	to specify color and size of clothing
6. names of clothing	to manage simple monetary trans-
7. money matters	actions
8. locations	to recognize basic terms of location

07   AT SCHOOL

1. names of school supplies	to recognize names of school
2. color, size	supplies
3. numbers *(hitotsu...)*	to specify color and size of school
4. names of school buildings	supplies
	to count objects
	to recognize school buildings

08   GOING TO THE ZOO

1. names of animals	to recognize names of animals
2. description: size, color, shape	to specify color and size of animals
3. likes/dislikes	to state preferences

09   HAPPY BIRTHDAY TO YOU

1. numbers	to state time of day, days of the week,
2. months of the year	days of the month, months of the
3. days of the month	year
4. days of the week	to state one's birthday (day and
5. time of day	month)
6. food and drink	to recognize names of food and
	drink

10   I HAVE A STOMACHACHE

1. facial features	to recognize facial features
2. parts of the body	to recognize parts of the body
3. description	

OVERVIEW OF CONTENTS

UNIT	TITLE	FUNCTION/OBJECTIVES	SONGS
0	INTRODUCTION	INTRODUCTION TO JAPANESE	
1	FIRST DAY OF SCHOOL	PRACTICING COURTESY EXPRESSIONS	SAYONARA GENKOTSUYAMA NO TANUKI-SAN
2	TELL ME ABOUT YOURSELF	DOING SELF-INTRODUCTIONS	
3	TELL ME ABOUT YOUR FAMILY	USING FAMILY TERMS	OHANASHI YUBI-SAN KOTORI NO UTA
4	DO WHAT THE TEACHER SAYS	FOLLOWING INSTRUCTIONS	TE O TATAKIMA-SHOO MUSUNDE HIRAITE
5	MY FAVORITE FOODS	DESCRIBING COLOR, TASTE, STATING PREFERENCE	AKAI TORI, KOTORI TULIPS
6	GOING TO THE STORE	NUMBERS 1-100	
7	AT SCHOOL	EXPRESSING POSSESSION	
8	GOING TO THE ZOO	EXPRESSING PREFERENCE, COLOR, SIZE	ZOO-SAN
9	HAPPY BIRTHDAY	EXPRESSING TIME	OSHOOGATSU
10	I HAVE A STOMACH-ACHE	RECOGNIZING PARTS OF THE BODY	MUSUNDE HIRAITE

GAMES, ACTIVITIES	VOCABULARY	EXPRESSIONS
		CLASSROOM INSTRUCTIONS
JAN KEN PON	-SAN, -KUN, HAI, SENSEI	OHAYOO, KONNICHIWA, KON-BANWA, YOKU DEKIMASHITA, ARIGATOO, DOO ITASHIMASHITE, GOMENNASAI, II YO
WHO IS THE LEADER?	BOKU, WATASHI, DARE, NAMAE, UN	
KARUTA	BOKU NO-, WATASHI NO, OTOOSAN, OKAASAN, ONII-SAN, ONEESAN, OTOOTO, IMOOTO, OJIISAN, OBAA-SAN, AKACHAN, KAZOKU	
CHARADES SILENT RELAY	BASIC VERBS	
MAGIC ENVELOPES BINGO VARIATION	KORE, SUKI, KIRAI FRUITS AND VEGETABLES OOKII, CHIISAI, NAGAI, MIJIKAI, OISHII, MAZUI, AMAI, SUPPAI	
FOUR-WAY BINGO MUSICAL CHAIRS	ARIMASU, IKUTSU, KUDASAI 1-100, HITOTSU-TOO, NAMES OF STORES	HAI DOOZO
MASTERMIND	SCHOOL SUPPLIES DARE NO, MOTTE IMASU KA	
	ANIMALS	
SNAKES AND LADDERS	-GATSU, -NICHI, -YOOBI, -JI, TOKEI, TANJOOBI, HARU, NATSU, AKI, FUGU, KISETSU, JAPANESE HOLIDAYS	
	ITAI, MIGI, HIDARI, SUKOSHI, SOKO SOKO, BODY PARTS	

A NOTE TO THE TEACHER

CLASSROOM INSTRUCTIONS:

Kiite kudasai.
Itte kudasai.
Ookina koe de itte kudasai.
Minna de (issho ni) itte kudasai.
Kazoete kudasai.
Kaite kudasai.
Nutte kudasai.
--nin guruupu o tsukutte kudasai.
Tatte kudasai.
Suwatte kudasai.
Kotchi e kite kudasai.
Mae e kite kudasai.
Utaimashoo.
Shizuka ni shite kudasai.

This is a list of high-frequency classroom instructions you will probably want to use from Day 1. Your goal is to be able to use them comfortably in class, without using English.

Your students should be able to *comprehend* what you are saying, but they need not be expected to *repeat* any of these instructions. In other words, these instructions are for *recognition only*. Also, it is not necessary to introduce them all at once. It is more natural to introduce and use them when a real need arises. However, just as every class has "rules" they must abide by, the instructions listed above may be considered "basic" classroom instructions.

"TIME ON TASK"

Based on the assumption that the average class has about 30 students, effective classroom control is necessary in order to make maximum use of limited class time. Therefore, depending on the number of students in your class, it may be necessary to modify the procedures described for some of the activities so that each student can spend as much time possible "on task": (i.e. actively participating in some kind of activity) instead of just passively listening.

The following chart (Ning, 1990) describes some of the various kinds of interaction patterns that are possible within a classroom. The two most common types of patterns are:

1) Teacher - class (choral response)   (Type 1)

   e.g.   Teacher: Ohayoo.
           Class: Ohayoo.

2) Teacher - individual student (one-to-one) (Type 2)

   e.g.   Teacher: Ohayoo.
           Ken: Ohayoo.
           Teacher: Ohayoo.
           Mary: Ohayoo.   etc.

It is suggested that Type 1 and 2 communication practice be used with discretion. Choral response is good as a "warm-up" activity and one-to-one response is good as a follow-up to that, but it is not necessary to do it 25-30 times in one session. It would be more effective to repeat the same drill the next day with a different set of students.

Many of the activities are Type 3. The teacher is still in control, all students are involved, and usually there is an element of competition among the small groups. *Karuta* is an example of a Type 3 activity.

Type 4 activities give small groups autonomy. The teacher's role is to move from group to group, checking to make sure that the activity is being done correctly and/or to answer questions.

Type 5 activities are paired-work activities. While this type of grouping maximizes each student's "time on task," it is the most difficult for the teacher to control since he/she will have to move around the classroom and check 12-15 pairs of students.

Patterns of Teacher-Student Interaction

Type 1

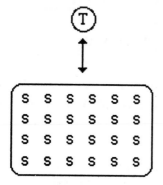

Type 2

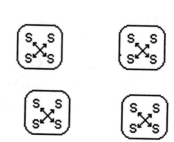

Type 3

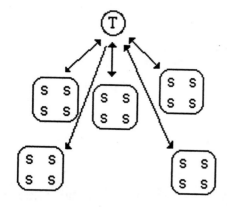

Type 4

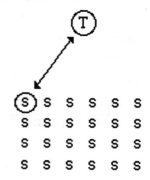

Type 5

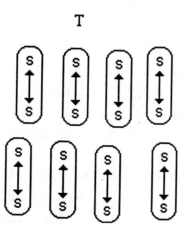

T= teacher

S= student

<---> = primary interaction

◯ = productive involvement

Adapted and modified from a chart devised by Cynthia Ning. Printed with permission from Cynthia Ning, 1990.

UNIT 1. *FIRST DAY OF SCHOOL*

OBJECTIVES: Knowing and using greetings.

USEFUL EXPRESSIONS: *ohayoo (gozaimasu), konnichi wa, konban wa, sayonara, yoku dekimashita*

DAY 1

Vocabulary: *ohayoo (gozaimasu), konnichi wa, konban wa, sayoonara, ~san, -kun, hai, sensei, yoku dekimashita*

Materials: puppet (any kind)
large visuals indicating morning, afternoon, and evening (1a)

Activities:

1.   INTRODUCING NEW VOCABULARY

Teacher acts out the following dialogue with a puppet, changing the tone of her voice, and introduces new vocabulary. A picture depicting morning (afternoon, and evening) is displayed on the blackboard (la).

    e.g.   Teacher: Ohayoo(gozaimasu).
           Puppet: Ohayoo(gozai)...I can't say
                      it!
           Teacher: Ohayoo.
           Puppet: Ohayoo.
           Teacher: Yoku dekimashita.
           Puppet: What's that?
           Teacher: It means "very good."

2.   ROLL-CALL: CALLING NAMES--1

Have the puppet take roll at the beginning of class.

    e.g.   Puppet: Sensei!
           Teacher: Hai.
           Puppet: Jeffry-kun!
           Jeffry: Hai.

1

Puppet:	Mary-san!
Mary:	Hai.
Puppet:	Tom-kun!
Class:	He's absent!
Puppet:	E?
Teacher:	Tom-kun wa kyoo oyasumi desu.
Puppet:	Tom-kun wa oyasumi?
Teacher:	Hai, soo desu.

3.   ROLL-CALL: CALLING NAMES--2

Teacher calls out one pupil's name, "Jeffry-kun." Jeffry answers, *"Hai."*
Then he calls his classmate's name "Lilibeth-san." Lilibeth answers *"Hai."*
The chain continues until everyone has had a chance to answer and call
someone.

4.   ROLE-PLAYING (PUPIL TO CLASS DRILL)

One pupil comes to the front of the class and selects a picture card
depicting morning, day (noon), or evening(1a). He shows it to the class.
The class says the appropriate greeting and the pupil responds. The
activity continues as pupils take turns going to the front of the class and
selecting picture cards.

e.g.   Anthony shows the class a picture of "morning."

Class:	Anthony-kun, ohayoo.
Anthony:	Ohayoo.

5.   SONG: *SAYONARA*

Sayonara, sayonara
Kore de kyoo wa owakare shimashoo
Sayonara, sayonara.

This song may be sung at the end of each day's lesson, to signal the
end of class.

DAY 2

Useful Expressions: *arigatoo, (doo itashimashite), gomennasai, ii yo.*

Materials: Puppet (any kind)
sets of nine cards each (one set per student) (lb)
several sets of 40 cards each (30 picture cards and 10 cards which have a picture of a pig on it) (1c)
picture card (1d)

Activities:

1.   INTRODUCING NEW VOCABULARY

Teacher acts out the following dialogue with a puppet and introduces *arigatoo*.

e.g. Puppet: Sensei, doozo. (puppet gives teacher something)
      Teacher: Arigatoo. Nan desu ka?
      Puppet: Akete mite (kudasai).
      Teacher: Waa...doomo arigatoo.
      Puppet: (Doo itashimashite.)

2.   GAME: *JAN KEN PON* (HOW MANY CARDS DO YOU HAVE?)

Divide the class into pairs. Each pupil is given ten cards.(lb) As each pair plays *Jan Ken Pon*, (see GAMES) the loser must hand over a card to the winner. The one who has more cards after X number of rounds is the winner.

e.g. both students say at the same time:
      " Jan Ken Pon."

Loser: Doozo. (gives winner a card)
Winner: Arigatoo.
Loser: (Doo itashimashite.)

3

JAN KEN PON:

This game resembles the "paper and stone" children's game where one extends an open hand (paper) or a closed fist (stone). A third motion is to extend the middle and pointer fingers (scissors). Each player calls out "Jan ken pon" and forms one of the above-mentioned shapes. Stone beats scissors, scissors beats paper, and paper beats stone. The game is played to determine who shall be "it" in games or who goes first or gets first choice.

3.   INTRODUCTION OF *GOMENNASAI*

Using picture cards (1d), introduce *Gomennasai*. Teacher can also act out with a puppet (by dropping it on the floor, apologizing, etc.).

4.   GAME: WHO DREW THE *BUTA*?

Prepare sets of 40 cards each (30 picture cards and 10 cards with pigs on them or some cartoon scene that evokes *gomennasai*)(lc). Divide the class into groups of five or six pupils. Place the deck of 40 cards, face-down, in the center of each group. The pupils take turns drawing a card from the pile. If a pupil draws a "pig" card, he must apologize to the others by saying *"gomennasai."* The others should say *"ii yo."* After all the cards are drawn, whoever has the most pig cards is the loser.

UNIT 2. *TELL ME ABOUT YOURSELF*

OBJECTIVES: Doing self-introductions and asking about others.

USEFUL EXPRESSIONS:
        Boku -- .
        Watashi -- .
        -- kun/ -- san
        Dare?
        Namae wa?

DAY 1

Useful Expressions:
        Watashi -- .
        Boku -- .
        Dare?

Vocabulary: *boku; watashi; namae wa? un*

Materials: puppets

Activities:

1. INTRODUCTION OF *BOKU, WATASHI, and NAMAE WA?*

   The teacher acts out the following with puppets.

   DIALOGUE 1

   Puppet 1: Boku, Gojira. Namae wa?
   Puppet 2: Watashi, Mimiko.
   Puppet 1: Issho ni asoboo.
   Puppet 2: Un.

2. ASKING NAMES-- 1

   The teacher asks each student his name.

   Teacher: Namae wa?
   Student A: (Boku wa) Jimmy (desu).
   Teacher: Namae wa?
   Student B: (Watashi wa) Mary (desu).

3. ASKING NAMES-- 2

   The teacher begins by asking one student his name with the question *"Namae wa?"* He answers *"Brad (desu.)"* The student then asks a classmate *"Namae wa?"* The second student answers, *"Amanda (desu.)"* The chain continues until everyone has had a chance to ask and answer the question.

5

DAY 2

Useful Expressions: ~ *san desu ka?*
~*kun desu ka?*
Hai./ Iie.
Dare ?

Vocabulary: *dare, ka*

Materials: pictures of famous people (movie stars, etc.)
students' own pictures taken about three years ago
puppet

Activities:

1. INTRODUCTION OF " ~ *SAN DESU KA?* "

The teacher acts out the following with puppets.

Teacher:	Gojira-kun desu ka?
Gojira:	Hai.
Teacher:	Mary-san desu ka?
Mimiko:	Iie.
Teacher:	Mimiko-san desu ka?
Mimiko:	Hai.

2. GAME: ~ *SAN DESU KA?*

The teacher shows the class pictures of famous people, asking "~ *san desu ka?* Students answer *"Hai."* or *"Iie."*

e.g.   (showing a picture of the current U. S. President)

Teacher:	Rinkaan-san desu ka?
Class :	Iie.
Teacher:	Kaataa-san desu ka?
Class :	Iie.
Teacher:	Bush-san desu ka?
Class :	Hai!

6

3. ASKING NAMES--3

The teacher points to one student and asks another student, *"Tom-kun desu ka?"* The student who is asked answers *"Hai"* or *"Iie."*

4. INTRODUCTION OF *"DARE DESU KA?"*

The teacher acts out the following with puppets.

Teacher:	(points to Gojira and says to Mimiko) Dare desu ka?
Mimiko:	Gojira-kun (desu).
Teacher:	(points to Mimiko and says to Gojira) Dare desu ka?
Gojira:	Mimiko-san (desu).

5. PASSIVE RECOGNITION OF NUMBERS

Arrange four or five large pictures of famous people on the blackboard, and number each one. Confirm that the students are familiar with each person by pointing and asking *"Dare desu ka."* Remove the pictures and put them in a different order. Then replace them on the blackboard, face down. Ask the students *"Ichiban wa dare desu ka."* If they guess incorrectly, respond by saying *"Iie, --san ja arimasen."* Continue the guessing game until all pictures are correctly identified.

The purpose of this activity is to passively introduce numbers before they are formally introduced in Unit 6. Other opportunities include counting off in Japanese and announcing individual and/or group winners in games and competitions.

6. GAME: *DARE DESU KA?*

Have each student bring a picture of himself or herself taken about three years ago. Show each one to the class, asking *"Dare desu ka?"*

Teacher:	(holding up a picture) Dare desu ka?
Class:	Tom-kun (desu).
Teacher:	(looking at Tom) Tom-kun desu ka?
Tom:	Hai.

(Variation--for competition) Divide the class into two groups. Show pictures of pupils in one group to the other group and have them guess who it is. Each correct guess earns one point.

DAY 3

REVIEW AND GAME

GAME: WHO IS THE LEADER?

One student is the detective and goes out of the room while the others form a circle. Teacher chooses one student (or a volunteer) in the circle to be the Leader. Detective returns to the room and stands in the center of the circle. Leader does some kind of action which the others mimic; for example--clapping his hands, hitting his left shoulder, winking his eye, etc. Every time he changes his action, others have to follow him. Detective must determine who the Leader is by asking *"H-san desu ka?"* Those in the circle can only answer *"Hai/Iie."* If the detective cannot determine the leader after five tries, he must ask *"Dare (desu ka)?"* Those in the circle will answer *"~ san (desu.)"* Leader becomes the next detective and the game continues.

UNIT 3. *TELL ME ABOUT YOUR FAMILY*

OBJECTIVES: Learning and using family terms.

USEFUL EXPRESSIONS: *Boku/watashi no ~ (desu.)*
-- no ~ (desu ka)?
Boku/watashi no ~ wa ~ (desu).
~ no namae wa naani?

VOCABULARY: otoosan, okaasan, oniisan, oneesan, otooto, imooto,
ojiisan, obaasan, akachan, kazoku.

DAY 1

Useful Expressions: *Boku/watashi no ~ desu.*

Vocabulary: otoosan, okaasan, oniisan, oneesan, otooto, imooto,
ojiisan, obaasan, akachan, kazoku.

Materials: fingerdolls (3a)
large pictures of family members (3b)

Activities:

1.   SONG FOR INTRODUCING NEW VOCABULARY: *OHANASHI YUBI-SAN*

Reproduce one set of fingerdolls for each student.(3a)   Have them cut
each doll out and tape each doll onto the appropriate finger, as illustrated.
Each verse is sung with that particular finger in an upright position. (e.g.
first verse is about father so point thumb "up.")

> This is my father, my chubby father
> yaa yaa yaa yaa wa ha ha ha ha ha ha
> He is talking with me.
>
> Watashi no otoosan, futoccho otoosan
> yaa yaa yaa yaa wa ha ha ha ha ha ha
> Ohanashi suru.
>
> This is my mother, my gentle mother
> maa maa maa maa o ho ho ho ho ho ho
> She is talking with me.
>
> Watashi no okaasan, yasashii okaasan
> maa maa maa maa o ho ho ho ho ho ho
> Ohanashi suru.
>
> This is my older brother, my big brother
> osu osu osu osu he he he he he he
> He is talking with me.
>
> Watashi no oniisan, ookii oniisan
> osu osu osu osu he he he he he he
> Ohanashi suru.

9

This is my older sister, my pretty sister
ara ara ara ara u fu fu fu fu fu
She is talking with me.

Watashi no oneesan, osharena oneesan
ara ara ara ara u fu fu fu fu fu
Ohanashi suru.

This is my younger brother, my naughty brother
nee nee nee nee e he he he he he he
He is talking with me.

Watashi no otooto, yancha na otooto
nee nee nee nee e he he he he he he
Ohanashi suru.

This is my younger sister, my cute sister
nee nee nee nee u fu fu fu fu fu fu
She is talking with me.

Watashi no imooto, kawaii imooto
nee nee nee nee u fu fu fu fu fu fu
Ohanashi suru.

2.   THIS IS MY FAMILY--1

The teacher brings a photograph of her family and introduces her family members to the class. *"Watashi no otoosan desu."*

3.   FAMILY TREE

Create a family tree on the blackboard with pictures (or draw free-hand)(3b) and ask *"Dare desu ka?"* . Review family terms.

e.g.   Teacher: (pointing to a picture) Dare desu ka?
       Class :   Otoosan (desu).

4.   DIALOGUE USING PICTURE CARDS (3b)

Jimmy: Otoosan ohayoo.
Otoosan: Jimmy ohayoo.
Jimmy: Okaasan ohayoo.
Okaasan: Jimmy ohayoo.

Jimmy: Oniisan ohayoo.
Oniisan: Jimmy ohayoo.
Jimmy: Oneesan ohayoo.
Oneesan: Jimmy ohayoo.

DAY 2

Useful   Expressions: *--kun/--san no ~ (desu ka)?*
(Boku/watashi no) ~ wa ~ (desu).

Materials: paper and crayons

Activities:

1.   DRAW A PICTURE OF YOUR FAMILY--1

Have each student draw a picture of his family, and have him introduce his family members to the class. *"Otoosan desu."* *"Okaasan desu."* etc.

2.   DRAW A PICTURE OF YOUR FAMILY--2

Using the pictures from Activity 1 above, ask the students, *"Anata no otoosan desu ka?"* *"Hai/Iie."* etc.

3.   THIS IS MY FAMILY--2

The teacher again shows a photograph of her family to the class and introduces her family members by name. e.g. *"Watashi no otoosan wa Kiyoshi desu."*

4.   DRAW A PICTURE OF YOUR FAMILY--3

Using the pictures from Activity 1 above, have the students introduce (the names of) their family members. e.g. *"(Boku no) otoosan wa Richard (desu.)"* *"(Watashi no) okaasan wa Cindy (desu.)"*

DAY 3

Useful   Expressions: *~ no namae wa naani?*

Vocabulary: *namae, naani (nan desu ka)*

Materials: some sets of picture cards of family members (3c)

Activities:

1.   DRAW A PICTURE OF YOUR FAMILY--4

Using the pictures from Day 2, ask each student, *"Otoosan no namae wa nan desu ka?"* As each student answers *" (   ) desu."* have him write the name of that family member under the picture.

11

2. GAME: *KARUTA* (RECOGNITION GAME)

Divide the class into groups of four or five students each. Give each group a set of picture cards (family members). (3c) Each set may contain more than one picture of each family member, so that students have more chances of getting a card. Face cards up in front of each group. When teacher says *"otoosan"* the first person who covers the correct card with his hand is the winner. Game continues until all cards are gone. The one with the most picture cards is the winner. Penalty system for covering the wrong card is left up to the individual teacher.

KARUTA:

This is a recognition card game using pictures, proverbs or words. Cards are spread out on the floor in front of the players. One person chooses a proverb at random and reads it (or some other appropriate cue) while the others try to find the corresponding picture card. The object of the game is to spot and seize the corresponding picture cards quickly; the player with the most cards wins. The children's version is used to teach *hiragana* and proverbs as well. These picture cards may have a character written in the corner or on one side.

3. SONG: *KOTORI NO UTA*

Kotori wa tottemo uta ga suki
Kaasan yobu no mo uta de yobu
Pipipipipi pipipipipi pichikuri pi.

Kotori wa tottemo uta ga suki
Toosan yobu no mo uta de yobu
Pipipipipi pipipipipi pichikuri pi.

UNIT 4. *DO WHAT THE TEACHER SAYS*

OBJECTIVES: Knowing and acting out simple daily activities.

USEFUL EXPRESSIONS: ~ *(si)te (kudasai).*

VOCABULARY: (Basic) *tatsu, suwaru, aruku, hashiru, tobu, mawaru, oyogu, kiku, neru, okiru, warau, okoru, naku, hanasu, utau, etc.*

(relates to Unit 5) *akaku nuru, aoku nuru, shiroku nuru, etc.*

(relates to Unit 7) *hon o hiraku, nooto o tojiru, kokuban o miru, enpitsu o dasu, pen o shimau, namae o kaku, kokuban o kesu, mado o akeru, mado o shimeru, doa o akeru, doa o shimeru, te o ageru, etc.*

(relates to Unit 9) *hanbaagaa o taberu, kokakoora o nomu, etc.*

(relates to Unit 10) *ha o migaku, kao o arau, te o arau, etc.*

DAY 1

Activities:

1. VOCABULARY INTRODUCTION (follow Total Physical Response Method)

   1) The puppet gives a command to the teacher in the target language and the teacher follows that command.

   2) The puppet gives another command and the teacher follows that command also.

   3) The puppet gives a third command and the teacher pretends she doesn't understand. She asks the puppet to repeat the command.

   4) The puppet repeats the command and this time the teacher follows the command.

   5) The puppet gives the same commands to the class, one at a time, then in a string of commands.

   6) The class and teacher follow the puppet's commands.

   7) The puppet changes the order of the commands.

13

8)   If a student makes a mistake, the puppet repeats the command.

9)   The teacher lets a student command the class, and the class follows accordingly.

2.   SONG: *TE O TATAKIMASHOO*

> Te o tatakimashoo, tantantan, tantantan,
> Ashibumi shimashoo, tantantantan, tantantan,
> Waraimashoo, ahhaha, waraimashoo, ahhaha,
> Ahhaha, ahhaha, aa omoshiroi.
>
> Te o tatakimashoo, tantantan, tantantan,
> Ashibumi shimashoo, tantantantan, tantantan,
> Okorimashoo, ununun, okorimashoo, ununun,
> Ununun, ununun, aa omoshiroi.
>
> Te o tatakimashoo, tantantan, tantantan,
> Ashibumi shimashoo, tantantantan, tantantan,
> Nakimashoo, enenen, nakimashoo, enenen,
> Enenen, enenen, aa omoshiroi.

This song may be sung with the class forming one large circle. Appropriate motions and body gestures should accompany each verse, for example, clapping hands, stamping feet, laughing, crying, etc. Change the actions and continue the song.

3.   GAME: CHARADES (GESTURE GAME)

Divide the class into two teams. Each team chooses one representative who acts out what the teacher says. The rest of the team tries to guess what their representative is doing. The team which guesses correctly first wins one point.

DAY 2

Activities:

1.   SONG: *MUSUNDE HIRAITE*

Musunde, hiraite, te o utte, musunde,
Mata hiraite, te o utte, sono te o ue ni,
Musunde, hiraite, te o utte, musunde.

Musunde, hiraite, te o utte, musunde,
Mata hiraite, te o utte, sono te o shita ni.
Musunde, hiraite, te o utte, musunde.

Musunde, hiraite, te o utte, musunde,
Mata hiraite, te o utte, sono te o mae ni,
Musunde, hiraite, te o utte, musunde.

Musunde, hiraite, te o utte, musunde,
Mata hiraite, te o utte, sono te o ushiro ni,
Musunde, hiraite, te o utte, musunde.

This song may be sung with the class forming a large circle. Appropriate motions and body gestures should accompany each verse. Change the actions and continue the song.

2.   GAME: SILENT INFORMATION RELAY

Divide the class into four or five teams, and have each team line up. The teacher whispers an action to the top batters of each line. They act out what the teacher says to the second person in line. The second student then motions to the third student and so on. The last person must tell the teacher what motion was being relayed. The team which relays the correct motion gets one point.

15

UNIT 5. *MY FAVORITE FOODS*

OBJECTIVES: Naming (fruits, vegetables, and other things)
Describing color, taste, and size
Stating preferences (for fruits and vegetables)

USEFUL EXPRESSIONS: *Kore (wa) ~ (desu).*
Naani? (Nan desu ka?)
~ (ga) suki (desu).
~ (ga) kirai (desu).

DAY 1

Useful Vocabulary: *Kore (wa) -- (desu).*
Naani? (Nan desu ka?)

Vocabulary: *ringo, banana, ichigo, suika, melon, painappuru, momo, mikan, ninjin, jagaimo, tamanegi, kyuuri, piiman, kabocha, etc.* (teacher should feel free to adjust this list)

Materials: pictures of fruits and vegetables (5a)
sets of card-size pictures of fruits and vegetables (5b)

Activities:

1.   INTRODUCTION OF FRUITS AND VEGETABLES

The teacher introduces the names of various fruits and vegetables using large visuals and/or real objects. (5a)

2.   GAME: *KARUTA* (MATCHING GAME)

See Unit 3, Day 3, Activity 2. Use sets of cards. (5b)

3.   *RINGO DESU KA?*

Showing a picture of a fruit or vegetable(5a), the teacher asks the class *"Nan desu ka?"* The class answers *"Ringo (desu)."*

DAY 2

Useful Expressions: *Akai ~ (desu).*
                         Akaku nutte (kudasai).

Vocabulary: *akai, aoi, kiiroi, shiroi, kuroi, chairoi, midori no, momoiro no, etc. , dore.*

Materials: Four picture sheets of birds (5c)
                one large and one small manila envelope
                paper circles of different colors
                student worksheets for coloring (5b)
                color by number worksheets (5d)
                words to song "Tulips" with picture to be colored (5e).

Activities:

1.   INTRODUCING COLORS

Tape four large picture sheets of birds(5c) on the blackboard.   While singing the following song, the teacher colors each bird, accordingly.

> Akai tori kotori, naze naze akai,
> Akai mi o tabeta.
> (Teacher colors the bird and berries red.)
>
> Aoi tori kotori, naze naze aoi,
> Aoi mi o tabeta.
> (Teacher colors the bird and berries blue.)
>
> Shiroi tori kotori, naze naze shiroi,
> Shiroi mi o tabeta.
> (Teacher colors the bird and berries white.)
>
> Kuroi tori kotori, naze naze kuroi,
> Kuroi mi o tabeta.
> (Teacher colors the bird and berries black.)

2.   GAME: MAGIC ENVELOPES--1

Prepare two manila envelopes--one large and one small--and put the smaller one into the larger one.   Cut out two circles about three inches in diameter of different colors.   Show them to the students and have them say each color.   Put one circle into the smaller envelope and the other into the larger envelope (without the students' knowledge).   Take the smaller envelope out of the larger envelope and ask them *"Akai? Aoi?"*   After each student makes a guess, the teacher takes out the colored circle from the envelope and shows it to the class.

17

3.   COLORING ACTIVITIES--1

Instruct students to color various objects on prepared worksheets(5b) specific colors. e.g. *"Ringo o akaku nutte kudasai."*

4.   IDENTIFY THE COLOR

The teacher displays pictures of various objects in different colors on the blackboard and asks *"Akai no wa nan desu ka?"* The students answer *"Ringo (desu)."*

5.   COLORING ACTIVITIES--2

Color by number.(5d) Distribute drawings (e.g. a boat in the lake, a house, etc.) that have been sectioned off and numbered 1- 4. Instruct the students to color all "1" areas red; "2" areas yellow; "3" areas blue; and "4" areas green. For example, teacher may say *"Ichi no tokoro, akaku nutte kudasai."*

6.   SONG: *TULIPS*

> Saita, saita, chuurippu no hana ga,
> Naranda, naranda, aka, shiro, kiiro,
> Dono hana mitemo, kirei da na.

Distribute the song sheets(5e) and have the students color the tulips according to the song.

DAY 3

Useful   Expressions: *Ookii ~ (desu).*

Vocabulary: *ookii, chiisai, nagai, mijikai, oishii, mazui, amai, suppai, etc.* (the teacher may add/delete to this list)

Materials: one large and one small manila envelope
pictures of various sizes of fruits and vegetables (5f)
worksheets for coloring (5f)
crayons

Activities:

1.   MAGIC ENVELOPES--2

See Unit 5, Day 2, Activity 2. Use pictures of fruits in various shapes and sizes (5f) instead of color circles.

2.   COLORING ACTIVITIES--2

Prepare worksheets to be colored (5f) and provide oral instructions for each picture. e.g. *ookii ringo o akaku nutte kudasai; chiisai melon o midori de nutte kudasai.*

3.   DESCRIBE THE FRUITS

Show a picture of a fruit and have the students describe it as much as possible. e.g. *Akai ringo (desu). Ookii ringo (desu). Amai ringo (desu). Oishii ringo (desu).*

4.   WHAT IS IT?

Prepare picture cards of fruit and vegetables(5b). Ask for a volunteer from the class. Have the student come forward and face his back to the rest of the class. Now show the class one of the cards. Pin the card on the student's back. The volunteer student does not know what he has but is allowed to ask ten questions of ten different class members. If the student does not get the correct answer after ten questions, the class may give him hints.

e.g.	Student:	Ringo desu ka?
	Class:	Iie.
	Student:	Ichigo desu ka?
	Class:	Hai.
	Student:	Ookii desu ka?
	Class:	Iie.
	Student:	Chiisai desu ka?
	Class:	Hai.

DAY 4

Useful Expressions:	*-- (ga) suki (desu).*
	-- (ga) kirai (desu).
Vocabulary:	*suki, kirai*
Materials:	puppets
	pictures of father and mother (3b)
	fruits and vegetables (5a)
	bingo cards (6d)

19

Activities:

1. INTRODUCTION OF ~ *(ga) suki (desu)/~ (ga) kirai (desu).*

Dialogue between puppet and teacher about mother, father, and puppet. Put pictures of father, mother (3b) and puppet on the blackboard.

Puppet:	Sensei, otoosan suki?
Teacher:	Hai, suki desu yo. (places a heart on father's picture.)
Puppet:	Okaasan mo suki?
Teacher:	Ee, okaasan mo suki desu yo. (places a heart on mother's picture.)
Puppet:	Boku wa?
Teacher:	Gojira-kun? A, sensei wa Gojira-kun ga daisuki desu yo. (places two hearts on puppet's picture.)
Puppet:	Yatta!

2. SONG: *KOTORI NO UTA*

See Unit 3, Day 3, Activity 3.

3. FRUITS AND VEGETABLES: ~ *(ga) suki (desu)/~ (ga) kirai (desu).*

Dialogue between puppet and teacher about vegetables, using real objects.

Puppet:	Sensei, jagaimo suki?
Teacher:	Hai, suki desu yo. Gojira-san wa?
Puppet:	Boku mo jagaimo ga suki. Sensei, kyuuri wa?
Teacher:	A, kyuuri mo suki yo.
Puppet:	Boku mo. Ninjin wa?
Teacher:	Ninjin? Ninjin wa kirai!

4. BINGO GAME--VARIATION 1

Put pictures of various (10-15) fruits and vegetables (5a) on the board. Distribute bingo cards (6d) and have each student draw in eight favorite fruits and vegetables among those pictured on the blackboard. Puppet goes around the class, announcing each student's favorite fruits and vegetables.

e.g.	Puppet:	Tom-kun, chotto misete... Aa, Tom-kun wa ringo to banana to ... ga suki desu nee.
	Tom:	Hai.
	Puppet:	Soshite, tamanegi ga kirai desu nee.
	Tom:	Hai.

20

5. BINGO GAME--VARIATION 2

Pair up students. Have them play bingo with the cards created in the above activity. (6d) Each student gets to mark a square if he gets a *"suki"* answer from his opponent.

e.g.   C   Mary-san wa ringo ga suki ? (Mary drew an apple on her card so she must answer "yes.")

        M: Hai, suki (desu).
(Cathy marks an X on her apple square.)

        M: Cathy-san wa orenji ga suki? (Cathy did not draw an orange on her card so she must answer "no.")

        C: Iie, kirai (desu).
(Mary cannot mark her own orange square.)

The game continues until one person makes BINGO according to the rules explained in Unit 6, Day 1, Activity 4.

UNIT 6: *GOING TO THE STORE*

OBJECTIVES: Recognizing #1-100
Counting #1-100
Learning names of shops
Managing simple monetary transactions

USEFUL EXPRESSIONS: -- *arimasu ka.*
Ikutsu arimasu ka.
-- *kudasai.*
Doozo.

VOCABULARY: 1 - 100; *hitotsu -- too*

DAY 1

Vocabulary: #1-20

Materials: two sets of number cards #1-10 (6a)
some sets of cards of different numbers of objects (6b)
worksheets for coloring, crayons (6c)
bingo cards (two rows of four blocks across) (6d)

Useful Expressions: Ikutsu (desu ka)?

Activities:

1.   INTRODUCING NUMBERS #1-20

Introduce numbers 1-20 using the number flash cards (6a).

2.   GAME: PICK UP THE NUMBER

Divide the class into five or six groups. Give each group a set of picture cards (6b). The teacher says a number (e.g. *SAN*) and each group must search for the picture card with the same number of objects. The first group to find and show the correct card receives one point.

3.   COLOR BY NUMBER

Distribute drawings (6c) that have been sectioned off and numbered 1-4. Instruct the pupils to color all "*ichi*" areas "*aka*"; "*ni*" areas "*kiiro*"; "*san*" areas "*ao*"; etc. For instance, you might instruct the class in the following manner: *ichi no tokoro o akaku nutte kudasai.*

4.   GAME: FOUR-WAY BINGO

Prepare pupil sheets with three bingo cards (6d) consisting of eight blocks each (two rows of four blocks across). Have the pupils fill in each block of the first card with numbers between 1-20. (Each block must be a different number.) teacher calls out numbers (at random, using master set of numbers) until one pupil has "bingo." There are four ways to win and each time the rules for winning may be changed:

                e.g.   1.   four-corner bingo
                       2.   center (four center blocks) bingo
                       3.   top row bingo
                       4.   bottom row bingo

The remaining bingo cards may be filled in with larger numbers, e.g. from 21-40; 41-60, etc. and played with the same variations.

DAY 2

Useful Expressions: *ikutsu arimasu ka?*

Vocabulary: #21-50, *ikutsu, arimasu*

Materials: two sets of number cards (6a)
                beans or anything else appropriate, a bag
                bingo cards (6d)

Activities:

1.   INTRODUCING NUMBERS #21-50

Introduce #21-50 using number cards(6a).

2.   GAME: HOW MANY BEANS?

Teacher grabs a handful of beans (or anything else appropriate) and puts them into a bag. Each student guesses how many beans are in the bag. The whole class counts out loud as the teacher takes the beans out one at a time.

3.   GAME: NUMERICAL "MUSICAL CHAIRS"

The students sit on chairs arranged in a circle and number off out loud, e.g. *"ICHI desu" "NI desu,"* etc. One student sits in the center of the circle. He calls out any two numbers. For example, if the student in the center calls out *"SAN to HACHI"*, students 3 and 8 should quickly change places. At the same time the student in the center tries to occupy one of their vacant chairs. If he succeeds, the player who now has no place to sit in the circle goes to the center and calls numbers.

4. GAME: FOUR-WAY BINGO--2 (#21-50)(6d)

Use bingo cards (6d) and refer to Unit 6, Day 1, Activity 4.

DAY 3

Vocabulary: #51-80

Materials: two sets of number cards (6a)
bingo cards (6d)

Activities:

1. INTRODUCING NUMBERS #51-80

Introduce numbers 51-80 using number cards.(6a)

2. FOUR-WAY BINGO--3 (#51-80)

Use bingo cards (6d) and refer to Unit 6, Day 1, Activity 4.

3. GAME: PETER IS CALLING PAUL

The pupils form a circle in which Peter is next to Paul and the others each have numbers. The game begins with Peter saying, "Peter is calling Paul." Paul replies by calling any one of the others, for instance, "Paul is calling *SAN*." No. 3 must then respond without hesitation and call someone else, e.g. *"SAN* is calling *GO."* So it continues, with each one called immediately calling another. Anybody failing to respond immediately goes to stand next to the one with the highest number. All the players then number off again, and some find themselves with new numbers. Peter and Paul can be called too. If they do not respond at once they must also move, and everybody moves up one. There is a new Peter and Paul, and everybody else counts off again.

DAY 4

Vocabulary: #81-100

Materials: two sets of number cards (6a)
                    bingo cards (6d)
                    game sheets for "Snakes and Ladders" (6e)
                    dice
                    playing pieces (1 per student)

Activities:

1.   INTRODUCING NUMBERS #81-100

      Introduce #81-100 using number cards (6a).

2.   FOUR-WAY BINGO--4 (#81-100)

      Use bingo cards (6d) and refer to Unit 6, Day 1, Activity 4.

3.   GAME: SNAKES AND LADDERS

      Divide the class into five or six groups.   Distribute "Snakes and
Ladders" game sheets.(6e)   Each player throws a die and moves his playing
piece along the number squares, counting aloud.   The sheet has rewards
and penalties.   Whenever a player's piece lands on a snake's head, he is
"swallowed" and has to go back to where the snake's tail is.   But whenever
it brings him to the foot of a ladder, he "climbs up" and is allowed to skip
the spaces in between.   The first person to reach the GOAL is the winner.

DAY 5

Useful Expressions: *Ikutsu arimasu ka?*
                          Futatsu arimasu.

Vocabulary: *hitotsu, futatsu, mittsu...too.*

Materials: number cards (6a)
                          beans (or anything else appropriate)
                          a bag
                          worksheets for coloring (6f)
                          crayons

Activities:

1.   INTRODUCING NUMBERS *hitotsu, futatsu, mittsu... too*

      Introduce this set of numbers using the number cards. (6a)

25

2. COLOR BY NUMBER--2

Prepare sheets with rows of objects (e.g. strawberries, cherries, apples, etc.). (6f) Teacher says a number and students must color the appropriate number of objects in that row.

3. HOW MANY BEANS?--2

See Unit 6, Day 2, Activity 2. Make the pupils answer by using *hitotsu, futatsu, etc.* instead of *ichi, ni, etc.*

4. SONGS: Sing songs like *TEN LITTLE INDIAN BOYS*, first in English and then in Japanese.

DAY 6

Useful Expressions: *~ (ga / wa) arimasu ka?*
(~ o) ~ tsu kudasai. Hai doozo.
Ikura desu ka.

Vocabulary: *kudasai, doozo*
names of various establishments: ginkoo, suupaa, yuubinkyoku, hanaya, toshokan, gakkoo, etc.

Materials: pictures of various shops (6g)
picture cards of various objects (ten cards per object) (5b)
shopping lists (6h)
coins (use poker chips, buttons, bingo markers - label)
price list (6i)

Activities:

1. INTRODUCING THE NAMES OF SHOPS

Introduce the names of various shops, with pictures. (6g)

2. SHOPPING--1

Divide the class into groups of two to three students each. Distribute three sets of picture cards (5b) to each group. Each set consists of ten pictures each of three different objects (e.g. ten apples, ten oranges, ten strawberries). Teacher goes "shopping" from group to group, practicing the following conversation:

Teacher:	(to Group A) Ringo(ga) arimasu ka?	
Group A:	Iie.	
Teacher:	(to Group B) Ringo (ga) arimasu ka?	
Group B:	Hai.	
Teacher:	Ringo (o) mittsu kudasai.	
Group B:	Hai, doozo. (hands three apple cards to the teacher)	

3. SHOPPING--2

Play the above game, adding the element of competition. Divide the class into two groups. One group forms smaller groups of "stores" and the other group forms smaller groups of "shoppers." Each "store" has "merchandise" consisting of three sets of different object cards (ten cards each). (5b) Each "shopper" has a "shopping list." (6h) The "shoppers" must visit the stores and try to buy the things on their list. The first group of shoppers to buy everything on their list is the winner.

4. PRICES OF OBJECTS

Using newspaper ads, ask the class how much various articles cost.

e.g.	Teacher:	Ringo wa ikura (desu ka)?
	Class:	60 sento (desu).
	Teacher:	Meron wa ikura (desu ka)?
	Class:	1 doru 25 sento (desu).

5. GAME: SHOPPING

Divide the class into teams of four to five students each. Each team receives 100 yen (use poker chips, buttons, or bingo markers) and a price list (6i) for the objects that they will sell. A representative from each team rolls the dice (or other appropriate object) and moves that number of spaces. He must buy whatever object is pictured on that space unless it is an object that his team is selling.

The first team to reach the GOAL is the winner. Any team that goes bankrupt along the way while shopping is eliminated.

Special markings on the game board (6j) are as follows:

B	=	Bonus; each team must pay the displayed amount to whoever lands on this space.
R	=	Return to "Start."
Y	=	Skip a turn.

27

Example dialogue between teams:

Team A: (lands on apple square) Ringo wa ikura
            (desu ka)?

Team B: (apple seller; checks price list) Go-en (desu).
            (Team A pays Team B five yen.)

Team A: Hai, go-en (desu).   Ringo kudasai.

Team B: Arigatoo. Ringo o doozo.

NOTE TO THE TEACHER:

A sample drawing of the gameboard is located in the appendix (6j).
The teacher will need to construct a large board based on the drawing. The
various fruits and vegetables should vary in color and size.

UNIT 7. *AT SCHOOL*

OBJECTIVES: Learning names of school supplies.
Describing color and size of school supplies.
Expressing possession.

VOCABULARY: various school supplies

DAY 1

Useful Expressions: *Dare no ~ (desu ka)?*

Vocabulary: *enpitsu, pen, kureyon, keshigomu, hon, nooto, tsukue, isu, kokuban, mado, to, kyooshitsu, etc.*

Materials: five or six large pictures of school supplies (7a) (or real objects)
sets of small visuals of school supplies (7b)

Activities:

1.   INTRODUCING SCHOOL SUPPLIES

Introduce the names of various school supplies, using whatever articles are in the classroom.

2.   GAME: "MASTERMIND"

Teacher arranges five or six large visuals (7a) (of objects) along the chalkboard, identifying each one orally.   Students must arrange their own cards(7b) in the same order.   The teacher then re-arranges his large visuals and places them along the chalkboard turned over, so that the pupils cannot see the pictures.   The teacher again identifies each one orally, and the students must arrange their own cards in the same order.   The teacher then turns each visual over so studentss can check their work. Paired/group activity is also possible.

3.   TOTAL PHYSICAL RESPONSE ACTIVITY

Combine school objects with more action verbs.   See Unit 4, Day 1, Activity 1.

4.   *DARE NO ENPITSU DESU KA?*

Gather one personal belonging of each student (e.g. pencil, notebook, etc.) and put into a big bag.   Take out one at a time, asking *"Dare no ~ desu ka?"*   Class answers *"Mary-san no ~(desu)."*   and Mary must answer *"Watashi no ~ (desu)"* before the teacher returns it to her.

29

DAY 2

Useful Expressions: Akai enpitsu o motte imasu ka?

Vocabulary: motte imasu

Activities:

1. *MOTTE IMASU KA?--1* (VARIATION OF **TPR**)

    Ask the class questions like the following:

    > a. *Akai enpitsu o motte iru hito, te o agete kudasai.*
    > b. *Kiiroi nooto o motte iru hito, tatte kudasai.*

2. *MOTTE IMASU KA?--2*

    Ask each student questions about his personal possessions, for example:

    > *Aoi hon (o) motteru (imasu ka)?*
    > *Akai pen (o) motteru (imasu ka)?*

    Proceed with this activity as a chain activity, having one student ask his neighbor a similar question and so on, until everyone has had a chance to ask and answer a question.

3. GAME: MUSICAL CHAIRS

    See Unit 6, Day 2, Activity 3.   Each student has a school supply such as a red pencil, a blue notebook, etc. The students sit on chairs in a circle. In the center there is one student who calls out the name of one school supply, for example, *akai enpitsu.* The students who have red pencils must change places and the student in the center tries to occupy one of the vacated chairs.

30

UNIT 8. *GOING TO THE ZOO*

OBJECTIVES: Recognizing names of animals.
Describing color and size of animals.
Stating preferences for animals.

DAY 1

Vocabulary: *neko, inu, nezumi, kuma, ushi, saru, tora, buta, zoo, kame, niwatori, etc.*

Materials: large visuals of animals (8a)
bingo cards (6d)
some sets of index-sized picture cards of animals (8b)

Activities:

1. INTRODUCTION OF ANIMALS

   Teacher introduces names of various animals, using large visuals (8a).

2. GAME: ANIMAL BINGO--1

   Using the same bingo format as in numbers (6d) (see Unit 6, Day 1, Activity 4) play bingo with animals instead of numbers. List all possible animals on the board and have each student draw in eight animals on their cards instead of numbers.

3. GAME: ANIMAL *KARUTA*

   Using index-sized picture cards of animals, play animal *karuta*. (8b) Divide the class into groups of four or five students each and give each group a set of cards. Each set may consist of one or two cards of each animal, so that more students may win.

4. *KUMA DESU KA?*

   Showing a picture of an animal (8a), the teacher asks the class, *"Kuma desu ka?"* The class answers *"Hai/iie."*

31

DAY 2

Vocabulary: review of adjectives, colors
suki, kirai

Materials: large visuals of animals (8a)
bingo cards (6d)

Activities:

1.   *NAN DESU KA?*

Showing a picture of an animal, the teacher asks the class, *"Naani? (Nan desu ka?)"*   Class answers *"Kuma   (desu.)"*

2.   GAME: WHAT AM I?

Prepare animal picture-cards (8b).   Ask for a volunteer from the class. Have the student come forward and face his/her back to the rest of the class.   Now show the class one of the animal cards.   Pin the card on the student's back.   The student now becomes that animal.   The volunteer student does not know what he/she is, but the class does.   He/she is allowed to ask ten questions of ten different classmates.   If the student does not get the correct answer after ten questions, the class may give him/her   hints.

e.g.	Student:	Ookii (desu ka)?
	Class:	Iie.
	Student:	Chiisai (desu ka)?
	Class:	Hai.
	Student:	Kuroi (desu ka)?
	Class:	Hai.
	Student:	Inu (desu ka)?
	Class:	Iie.
	Student:	Neko (desu ka)?
	Class:	Hai!

You can also have competition among teams.

3. ~ *GA SUKI DESU KA?*

Give the class simple commands like " ~ *ga suki na hito, te o agete (kudasai.)"* Then ask each student *"~ ga suki desu ka?"*

e.g. Teacher: Neko ga suki na hito, te o agete (kudasai).
      Class: (responds by raising their hands)
      Teacher: Inu ga suki na hito, te o agete (kudasai).
      Class: (responds by raising their hands)

      Teacher: Uma ga suki desu ka?
      Student A: Hai.
      Student B: Iie.

4. GAME: ANIMAL BINGO--2

Use the bingo cards. (6d) List all possible animals on the board and have each student draw in eight favorite animals. Make students form pairs. Student A chooses one animal from his bingo card and asks Student B, *"Kuma ga suki desu ka?"* If B has a picture of a bear on his own bingo card, he answers *"Hai."* Then Student A can cross out his own bear picture on his card. The student who first gets four crossed-out boxes according to the bingo rules (see Unit 6, Day 1, Activity 4) wins.

5. SONG: *ZOO-SAN* (ELEPHANT SONG)

Zoo-san, Zoo-san, ohana ga nagai no ne.
Soo yo, kaasan mo nagai no yo.

Zoo-san, Zoo-san dare ga suki na no
Ano ne kaasan ga suki na no yo.

6. IMITATING ANIMAL SOUNDS

Play a game of "identify the animal" by imitating animal sounds (first in English and then in Japanese). Sing English songs like *OLD MACDONALD HAD A FARM* and then try a Japanese version of it.

UNIT 9. *HAPPY BIRTHDAY*

OBJECTIVES: Stating month of the year.
Stating day of the month.
Stating days of the week.
Stating time of day.
Stating one's birthday.

USEFUL EXPRESSIONS:
Nangatsu (desu ka)?   ~ gatsu (desu.)
Nannichi (desu ka)? ~ nichi (desu).
Nanyoobi (desu ka)? ~ yoobi (desu.)
Nanji (desu ka)? ~ ji (desu).
Watashi/boku no tanjoobi wa ~ gatsu
~ nichi (desu).

VOCABULARY: *--gatsu; --nichi; --yoobi; --ji; tanjoobi*

DAY 1

Useful Expressions: *Nangatsu (desu ka)?   ~gatsu (desu.)*
~ wa ~ gatsu (desu.)

Vocabulary: *gatsu, nangatsu, haru, natsu , aki, fuyu, kisetsu*

Materials: calendar
kanji cards (9a)
large visuals of American holidays and activities
associated with each month (9b)
large visuals of Japanese holidays and activities
associated with each month (9c)

Activities:

1. INTRODUCING EACH MONTH

Teacher introduces each month using a large calendar displayed on the blackboard.

e.g. Teacher: Ichigatsu desu. (pointing to January)
Nigatsu desu. (pointing to February)

2. *"ICHIGATSU DESU KA?"*

Pointing to the calendar, teachers asks *"Ichigatsu (desu ka)?"* Students should answer *"Hai/iie."*

3. *"NANGATSU DESU KA?"*

Pointing to the calendar, teachers asks *"Nan gatsu (desu ka)?"* Students should answer *"Ichigatsu (desu)."*

4. *KANJI* FLASH CARDS

Repeat activities 1 - 3 with the *kanji* flash cards (9a).

5. INTRODUCING ACTIVITIES (HOLIDAYS/SEASONS)

Teacher introduces the activities (holidays/seasons) associated with each month, using visuals (9b).

    e.g.   New Year's wa ichigatsu desu.
            Valentine's Day wa nigatsu desu. etc.

6. *"VALENTINE'S DAY WA SANGATSU DESU KA?"*

Holding up each visual, ask the class *"New Year's wa ichigatsu desu ka?"* Students should answer *"Hai/iie."*

7. *"VALENTINE'S DAY WA NANGATSU DESU KA?"*

Holding up each visual, ask the class *"New Year's wa nangatsu desu ka?"* Students should answer *"Ichigatsu (desu)."*

DAY 2

Vocabulary: oshoogatsu, setsubun, hinamatsuri, nyuugakushiki, kodomo no hi, tsuyu, tanabata, obon, tsukimi, undookai, shichigosan, mochitsuki

Materials: calendar
kanji cards (9a)
large visuals of Japanese activities associated with each month (9c)

Activities:

1. Repeat activities 5, 6, and 7 of Day 1 with visuals depicting Japanese holidays and activities.

2.   SONG: *OSHOOGATSU*

   Moo ikutsu neru to oshoogatsu
   Oshoogatsu niwa tako agete
   Koma o mawashite asobimashoo
   Hayaku koi koi oshoogatsu

   NOTE: Popular English songs, like *SILENT NIGHT*, can also be sung
   in Japanese.

DAY 3

Useful Expressions: ~ *wa nannichi (desu ka)?* ~ *nichi (desu).*

Vocabulary: *nichi, nannichi, tsuitachi, futsuka...tooka*

Materials: number flash cards (6a)
                kanji cards (9a)
                Snakes and Ladders game sheet (6e)

Activities:

1.   REVIEW NUMBERS

   Review numbers 1 - 31 and *hitotsu - too* using number cards. (6a)

2.   INTRODUCING *TSUITACHI - TOOKA*

   Introduce *tsuitachi - tooka* using a calendar and *kanji* flash cards.
(9a)

3.   GAME: SNAKES AND LADDERS

   Play Snakes and Ladders by saying the days of the month. (6e)   Refer
to Unit 6, Day 4, Activity 3.

36

4.   GAME: LET'S LINE UP!

Divide the class into three or four groups. Have members of each group line up in chronological order according to their birthdays. First group to line up accurately is the winner. They must be able to say their birthdays in Japanese.

DAY 4

Useful Expressions: *Kyoo wa nanyoobi (desu ka)?   ~yoobi (desu).*

Vocabulary: *Nichiyoobi, getsuyoobi, kayoobi, suiyoobi, mokuyoobi, kinyoobi, doyoobi, nanyoobi*

Materials: large *kanji* flash cards (9a)
calligraphy equipment: brush *(fude)*, ink, paper, old newspaper
small flash cards (9d)
kanji worksheets (9e)

Activities:

1.   INTRODUCTION OF THE DAYS OF THE WEEK

Introduce the days of the week using large *kanji* visuals. (9a) Explain the meanings of the individual characters and how some of the characters evolved from pictures of the objects they represent.

2.   CALLIGRAPHY PRACTICE

Provide each student with brush, paper, and ink. Protect the desks with lots of old newspaper. Display sample characters on the blackboard so that everyone may see them and use them as models.   If such equipment is not readily available, prepare worksheets (9e) for students to practice writing.

3.   GAME: *KANJI KARUTA*

Divide the class into groups of four-five students each. Give each group a set of *kanji* flash cards(9d) (may consist of two cards of each character) and play *karuta* in the usual manner.

DAY 5

Useful Expressions: *Nanji (desu ka)?* ~ *ji (desu.)*

Vocabulary: *ichiji - juuniji, nanji, tokei*

Materials: large manually operated clock
small manually operated clocks (for students)
clock worksheets (9f)
kanji cards (9a)

Activities:

1. REVIEW NUMBERS

Review numbers one to twelve.

2. *SANJI DESU YO.*

Practice saying the hours with a large manually operated clock.

3. LET'S SET THE TIME

Provide each student with his own clock (face and hands) and practice setting the time and telling time.

4. *NANJI DESU KA?*

Provide students with worksheets consisting of clock faces (9f) and have them draw in the hands according to oral directions.

38

UNIT 10. *I HAVE A STOMACHACHE*

OBJECTIVES: Recognizing facial features and parts of the body.

USEFUL EXPRESSIONS: ~ *ga itai* .

DAY 1

Useful Expressions: *motto migi, sukoshi hidari, soko soko*

Vocabulary: me, mimi, hana, kuchi, atama, kao, kubi, kata, ude, te, yubi, mune, senaka, oshiri, ashi, etc.

Materials: blindfold
pictures of various facial parts (10a)

Activities:

1. INTRODUCING NEW VOCABULARY

Have a volunteer come to the front of the class. Introduce the words for each facial part (or part of the body).

2. GAME: *FUKUWARAI*

Draw the outline of a face on the blackboard. Have one student come up to the front of the class and blindfold him. Select a picture of one part of the face (e.g. eye) (10a) and ask the class what it is. The class answers aloud so that the blindfolded student knows what it is. He then tries to place it in the proper position within the "face" on the blackboard. The other students can direct him by giving hints like *motto migi, sukoshi hidari, soko soko,* etc. Students take turns until a complete "face" has been produced.

3. GAME: DRAWING FACES

Prepare cards with pictures of various facial parts. (10a) Have a student pull one from the stack and tell the class what it is. The rest of the class must draw that particular part on their worksheets. Students take turns pulling cards until they are all gone.

39

DAY 2

Useful Expressions: ~ *ga itai.*

Vocabulary: *itai*

Materials: pictures of body parts (10b)
pictures of three faces with very different characteristics
pictures of outlines of three different faces
pictures of facial parts of three different faces
*these materials are not provided; teacher must draw her own.

Activities:

1. GAME: JIGSAW PUZZLE

Show the class pictures of three faces with very different characteristics and give each a name. (e.g. a girl with a round face, a man with a square face, and a lady with an oval face) Also prepare cards of each facial part of each face and mix them all up. Draw the outline of each face on the blackboard. Randomly select a card and show it to the class asking *"Dare no me desu ka?"* The class should respond *" ~ san no me (desu)."* Then place the card in its proper position on the appropriate face.

2. SONG: *MUSUNDE HIRAITE*

See Unit 4, Day 2, Activity 1. Change the underlined part into facial or body parts and make the students act it out while singing.

e.g.   *"sono te o <u>ue</u> ni"* may be changed to
"sono te o <u>mimi (atama, kata)</u> ni"

3. INTRODUCING *~GA ITAI.*

Introduce ~ *ga itai* using gestures, pretending to have an ache or pain somewhere.

4. GAME: CHARADES

Divide the class into two groups. One student of Group A comes to the front of the class and pretends that some part of his body is aching. The rest of his team must guess which part by saying *" ~ ga itai."* If they guess correctly, Group A gets one point. Then Group B does the same but with a different part of the body.

8:00 AM

9:00 PM

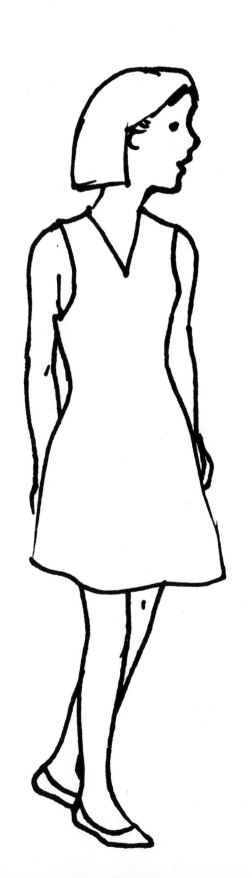

1a-43

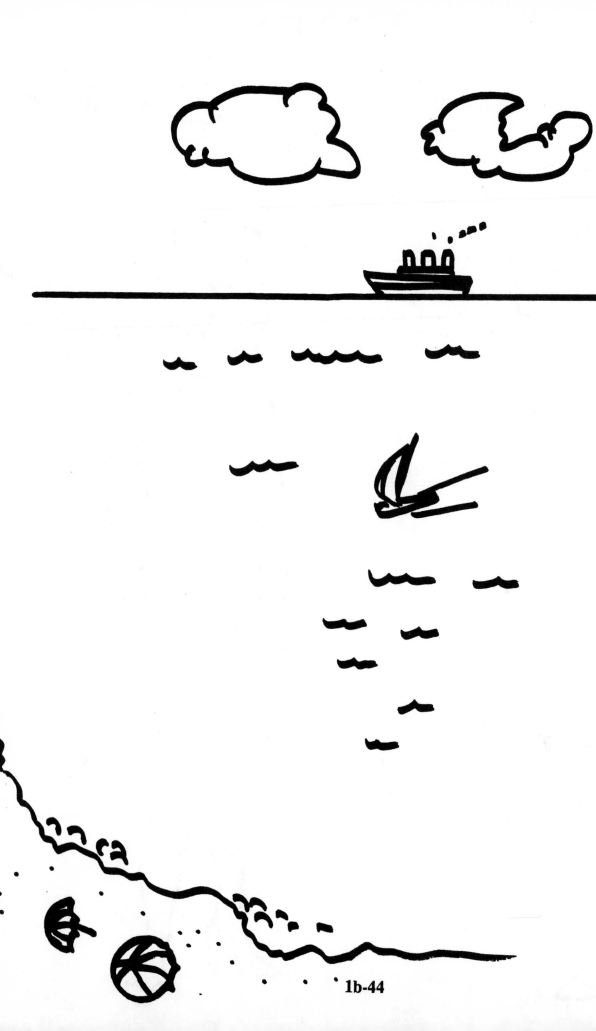

1b-44

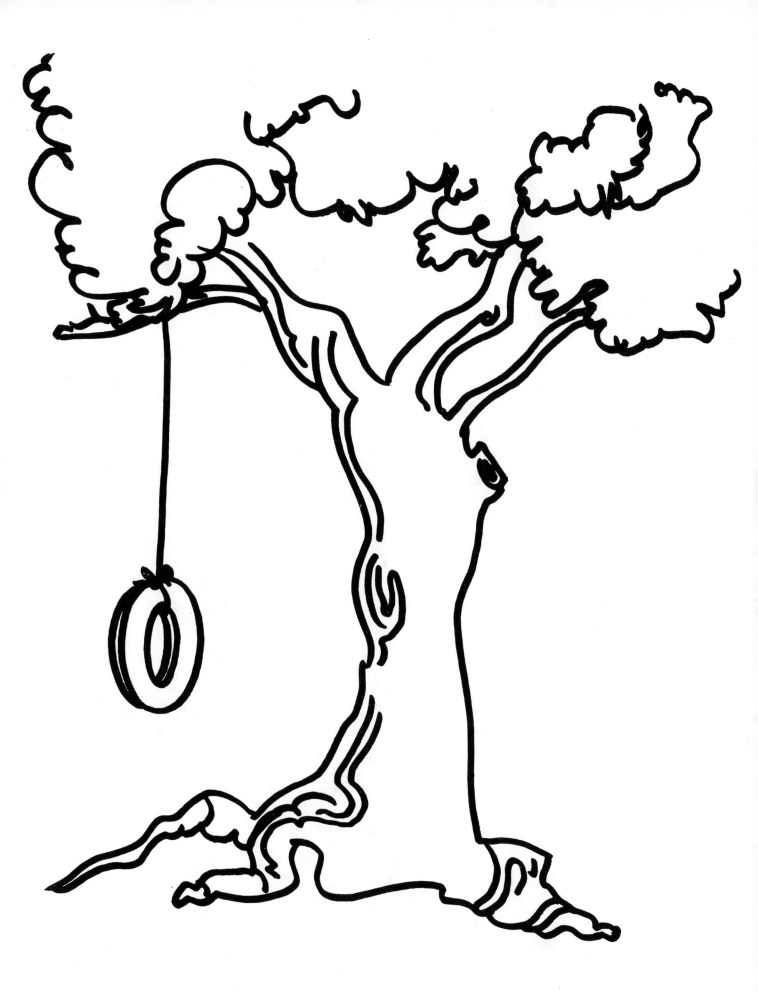

1b-46

1b-47

1b-53

OHANASHI YUBI-SAN

3b-59

3b-60

3b-66

5a-70

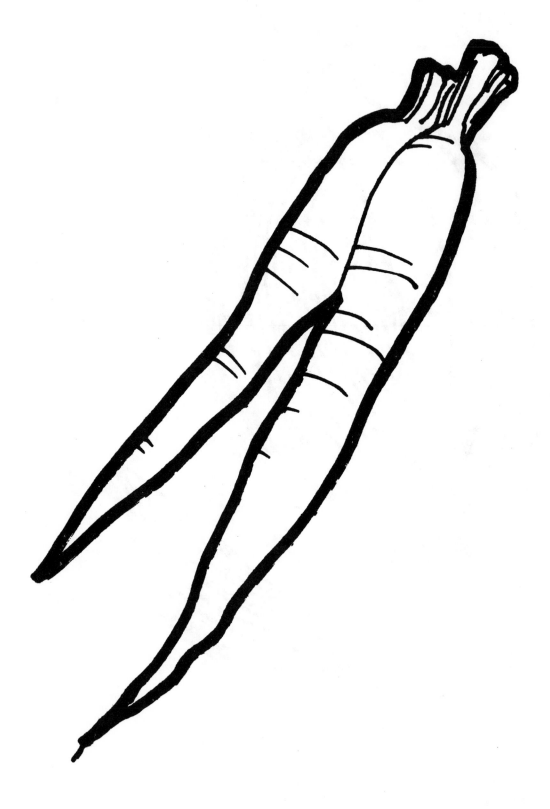

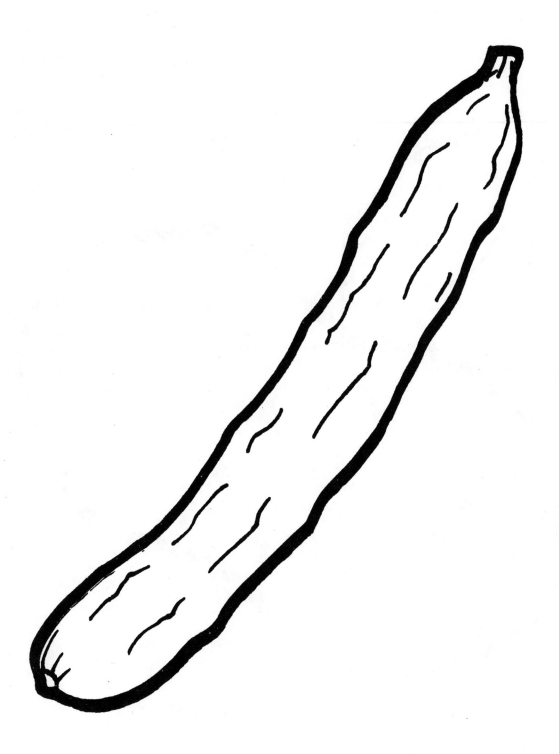

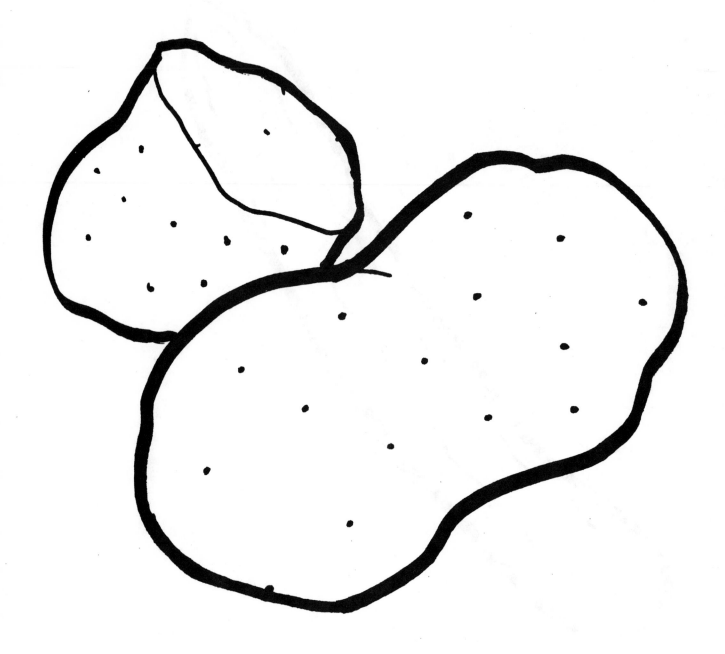

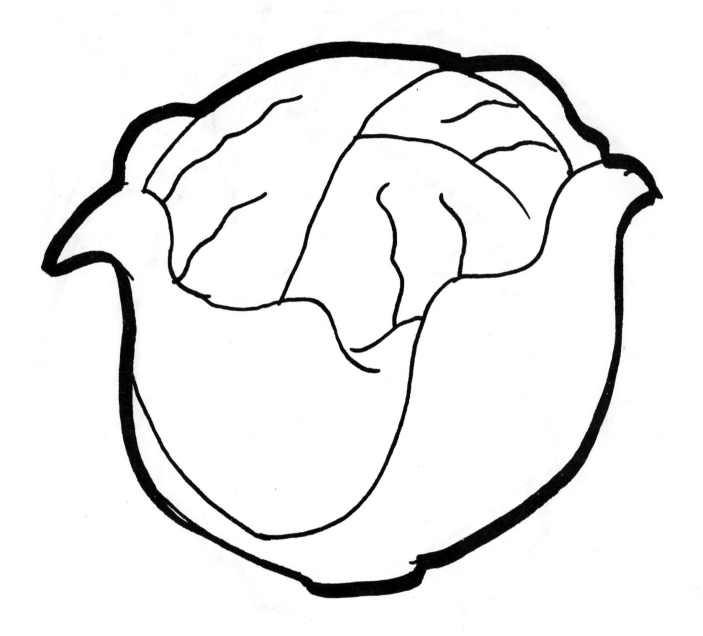

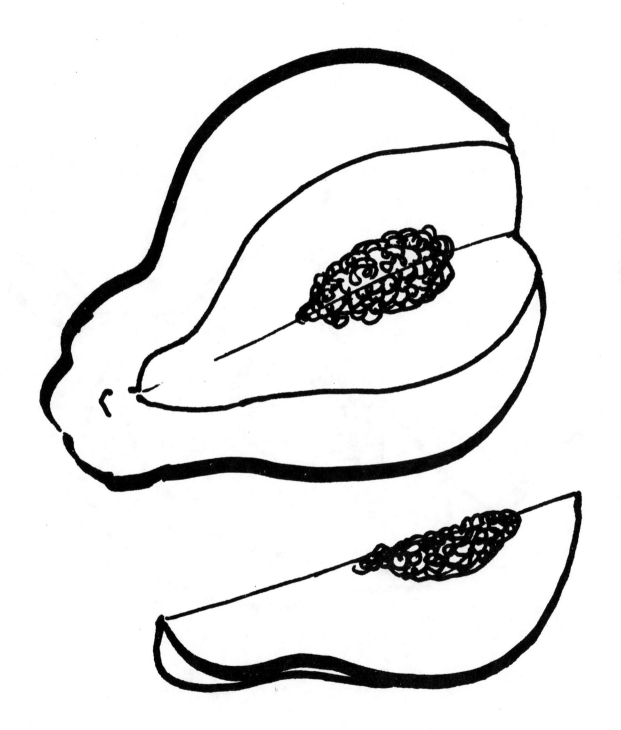

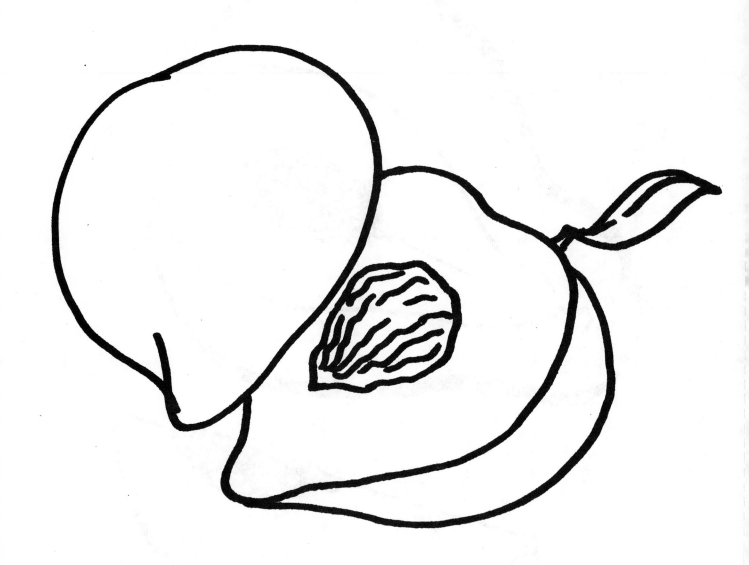

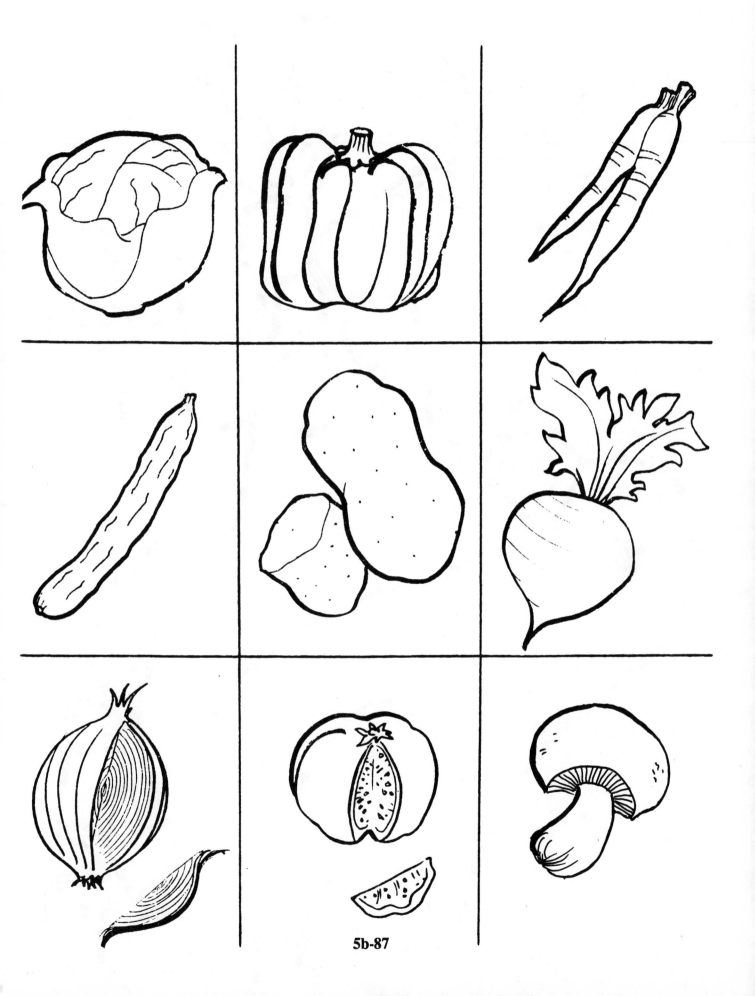

5b-87

5c-88

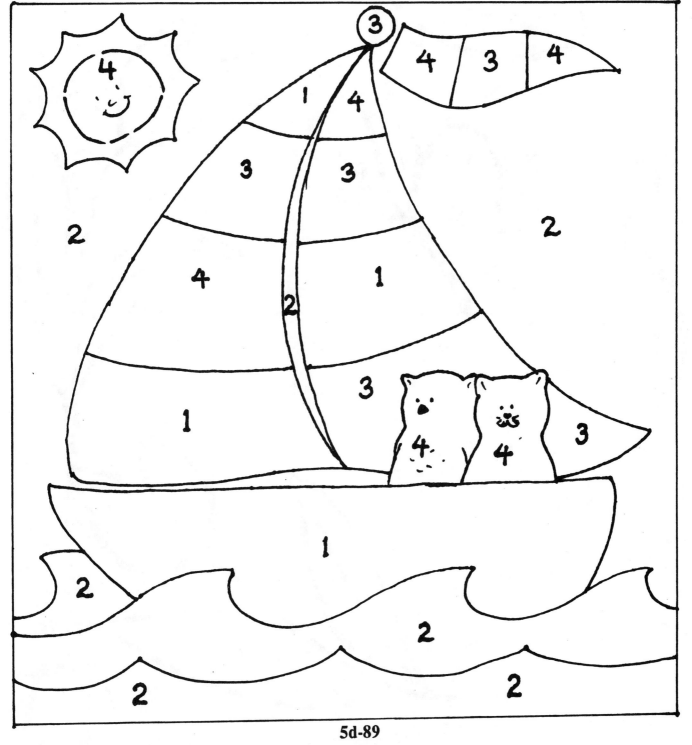

5f-91

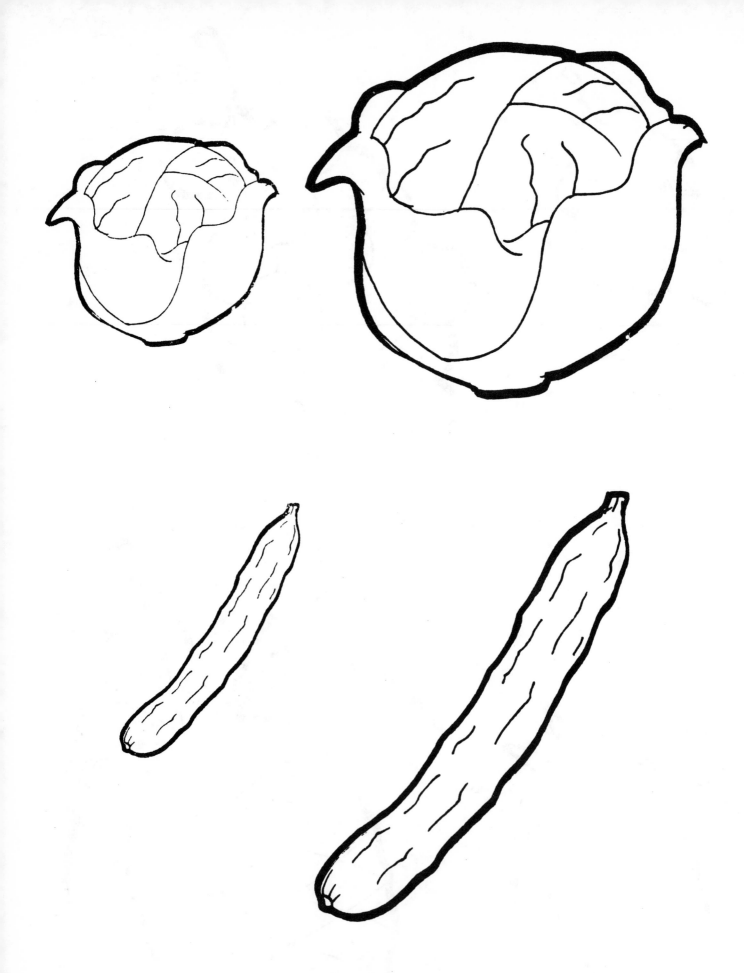

5f-94

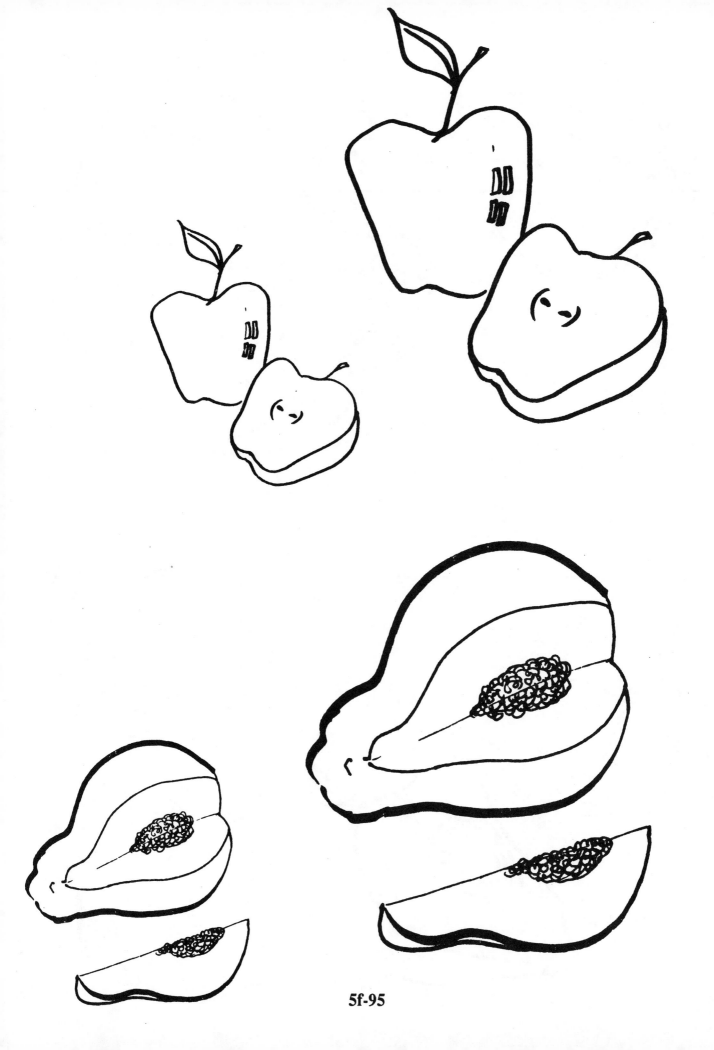

5f-95

5f-97

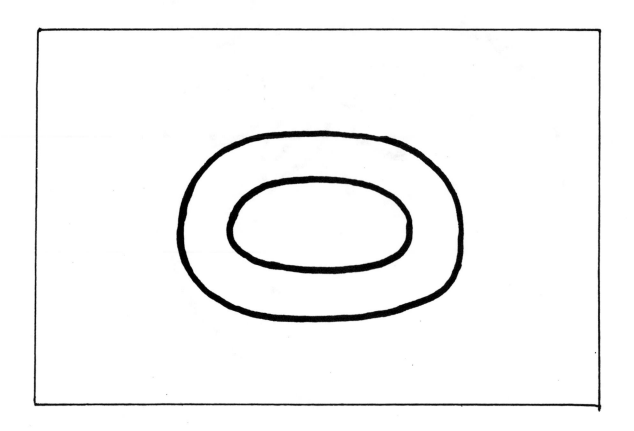

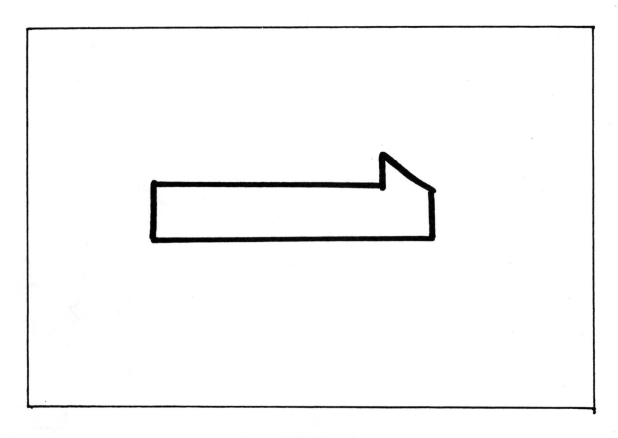

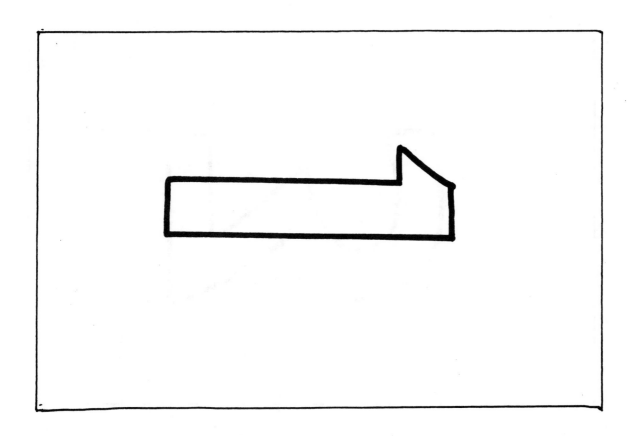

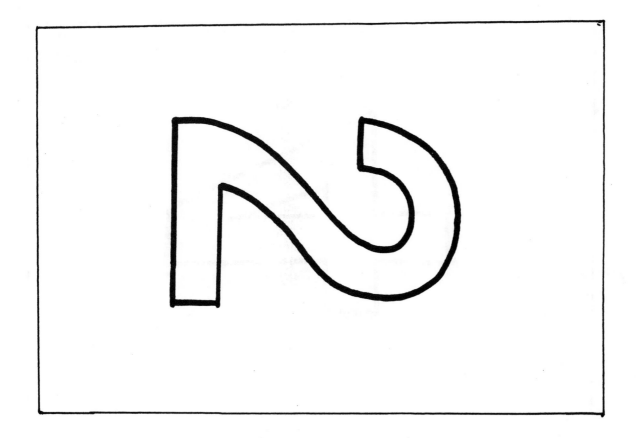

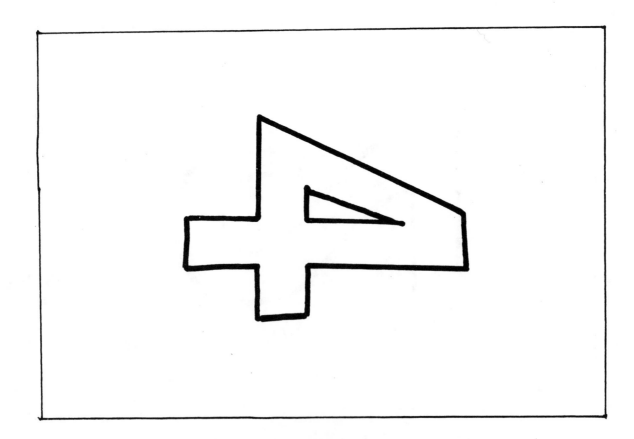

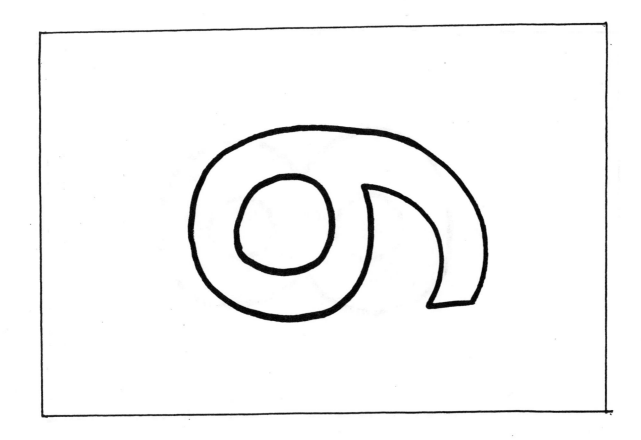

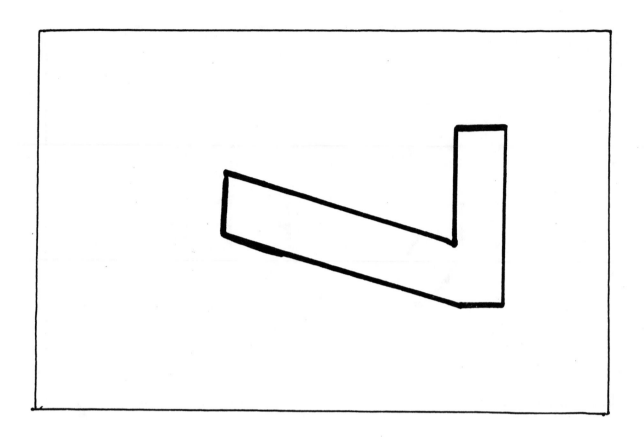

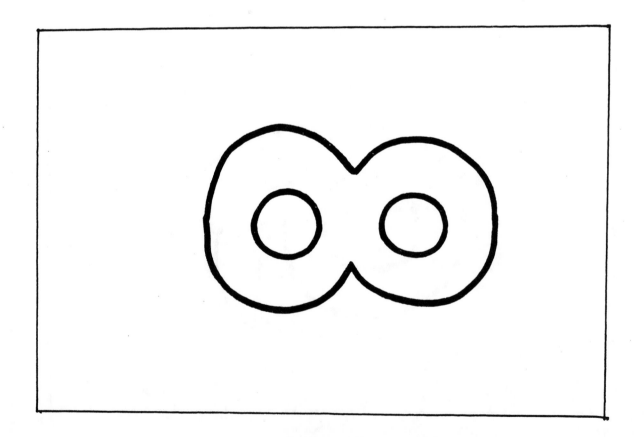

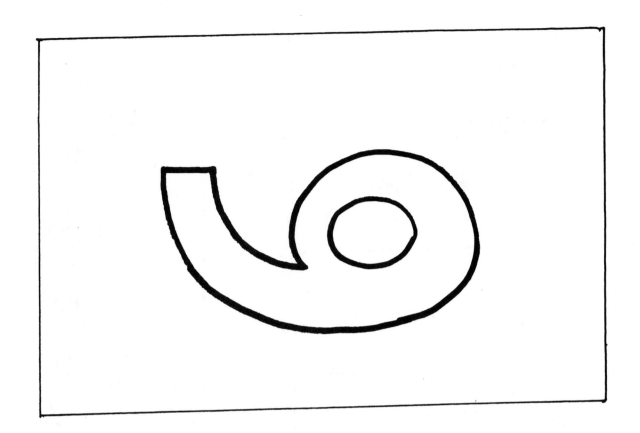

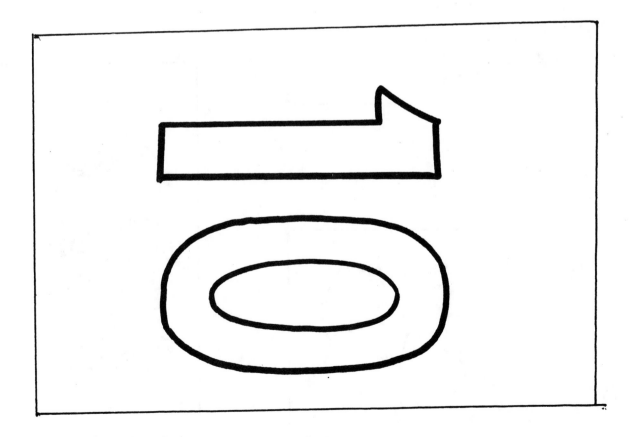

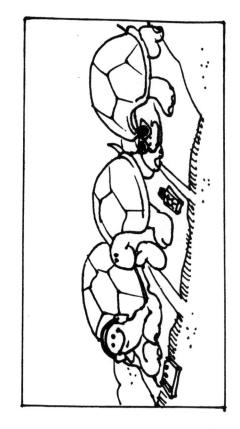

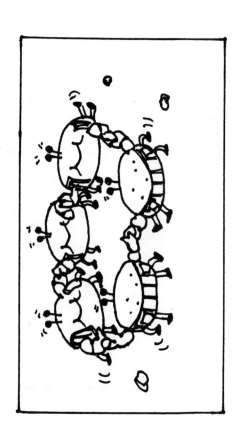

6b-104

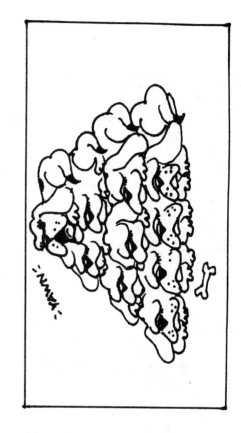

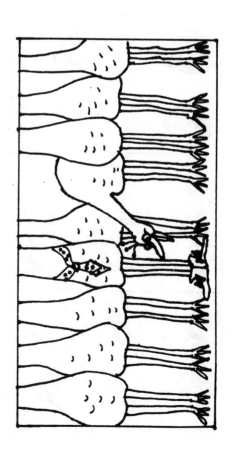

6b-105

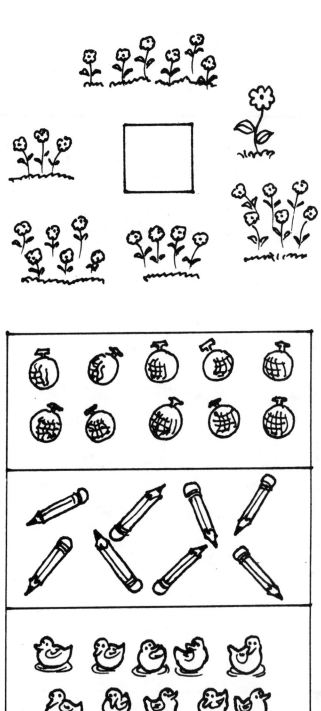

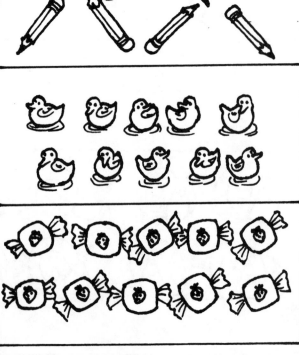

BINGO CARDS

goal
31
25 26 27 28 29 30
24 23 22 21 20 19
13 14 15 16 17 18
12 11 10 9 8 7
1 2 3 4 5 6
start

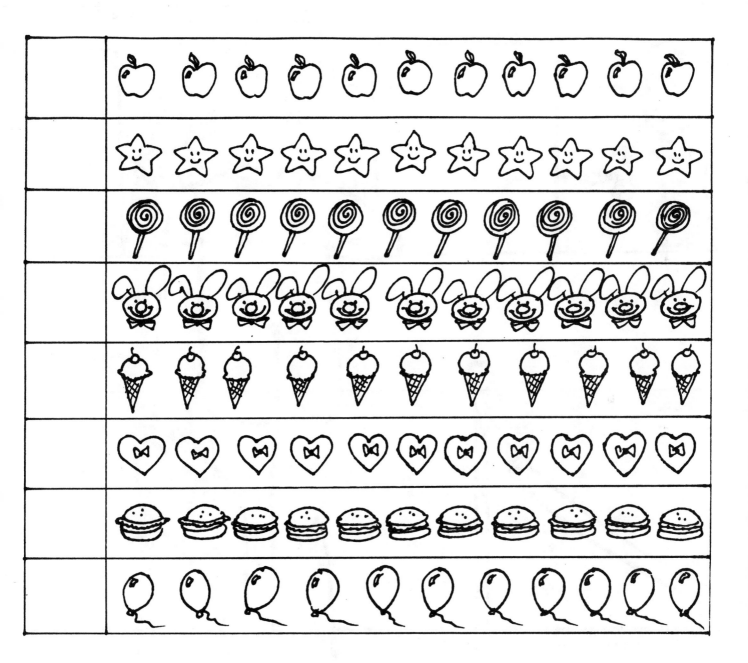

SHOPPING LISTS

SHOPPING LIST #1

2   apples
1   orange
1   pineapple
3   melons

SHOPPING LIST #2

4   potatoes
5   onions
2   tomatoes
1   cabbage

SHOPPING LIST #3

3   apples
1   onion
5   oranges
2   tomatoes

SHOPPING LIST #4

6   pineapples
1   watermelon
3   papayas
4   strawberries

NEDANHYOO

GROUP 1

5   YEN

10   YEN

15   YEN

20   YEN

25   YEN

GROUP 3

5   YEN

10   YEN

15   YEN

20   YEN

25   YEN

GROUP 2

5   YEN

10   YEN

15   YEN

20   YEN

25   YEN

GROUP 4

5   YEN

10   YEN

15   YEN

20   YEN

25   YEN

GROUP 5

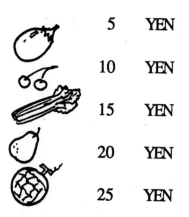

5   YEN

10   YEN

15   YEN

20   YEN

25   YEN

DIAGRAM OF SAMPLE GAMEBOARD

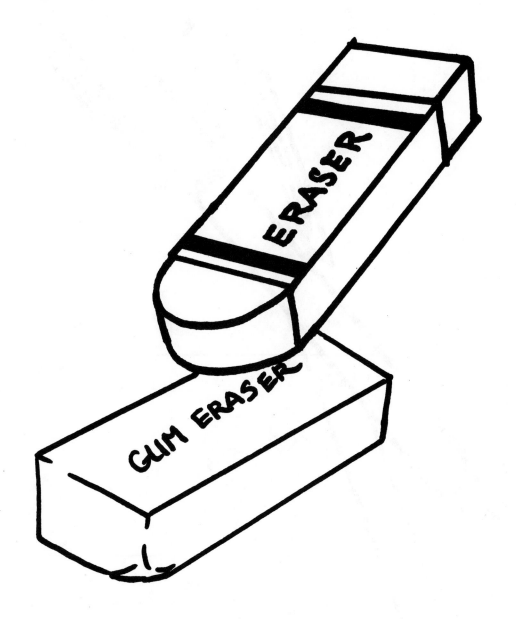

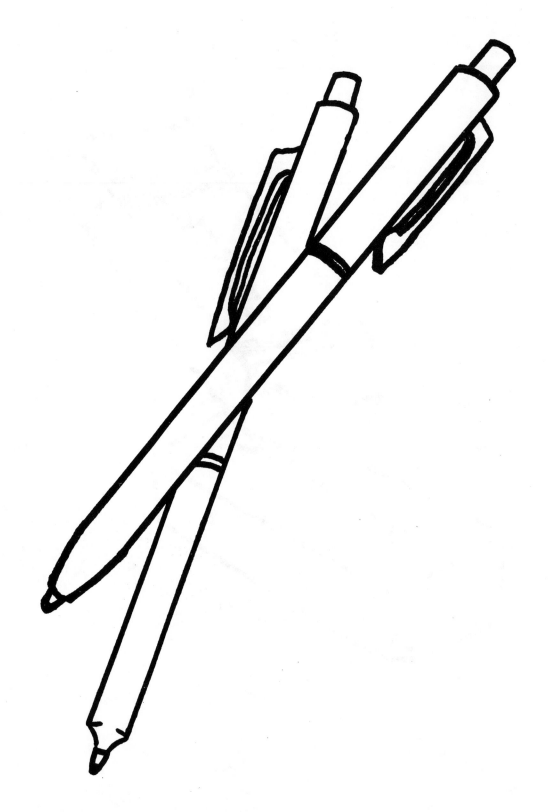

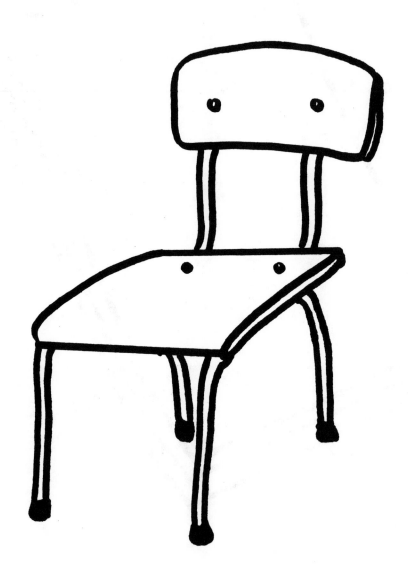

ERASER

NOTES

7b-126

8a-128

8a-129

8a-130

8a-132

8a-133

8a-134

8a-136

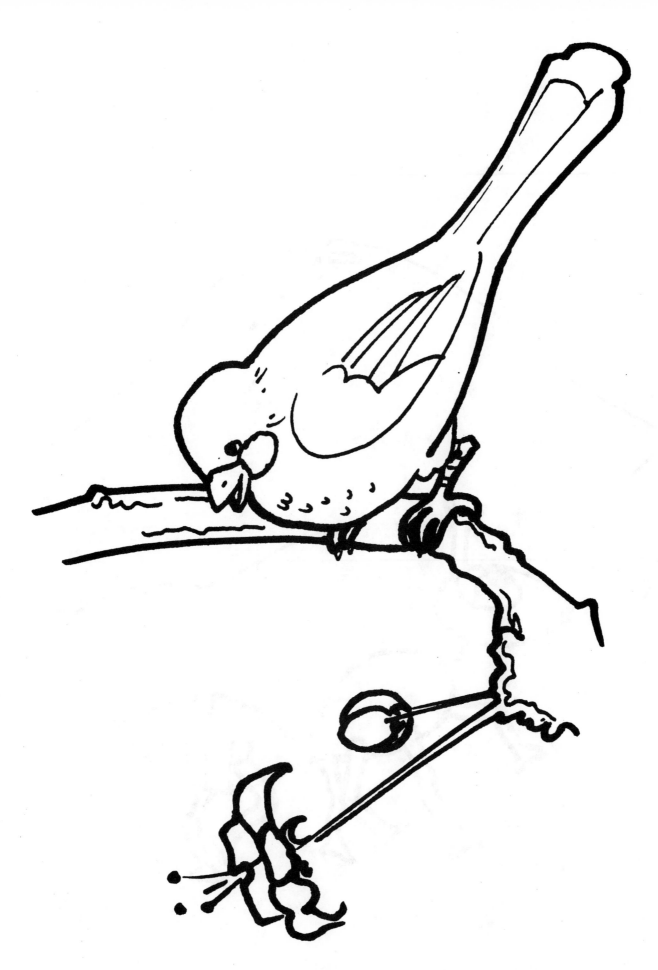

8a-137

8a-144

8a-150

8b-151

9a-152

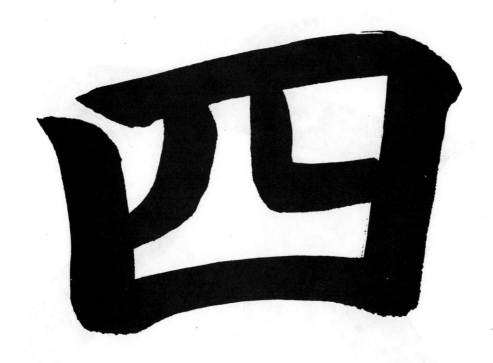

9a-154

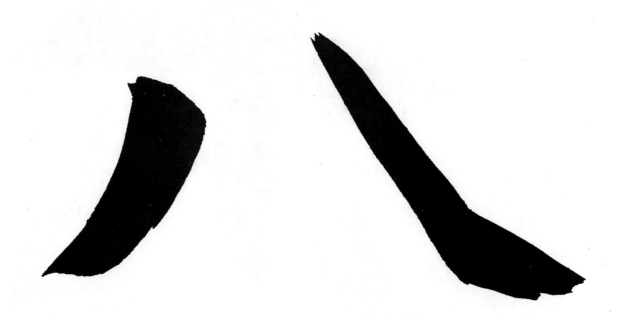

9a-156

9a-157

9a-161

9a-163

HAPPY NEW YEAR

9b-165

9b-166

9b-167

9c-169

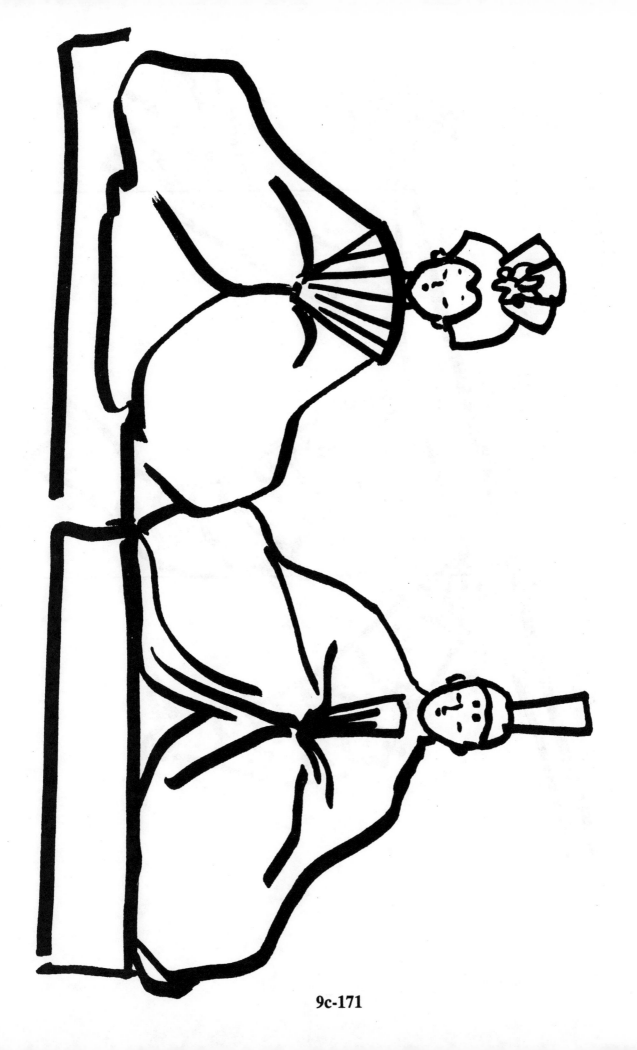

9c-171

一	二	三
四	五	六
七	八	九
十	日	時

月	火	水
木	金	土
春	夏	秋
冬	山	川

六 五 四 三 二 一

川 山 十 九 八 七

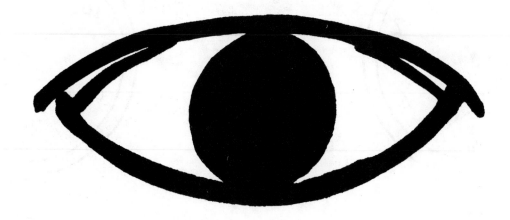

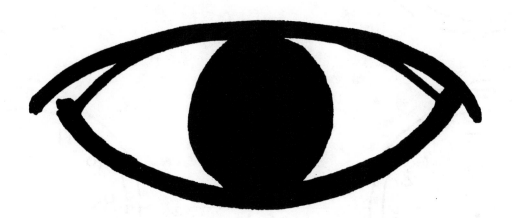

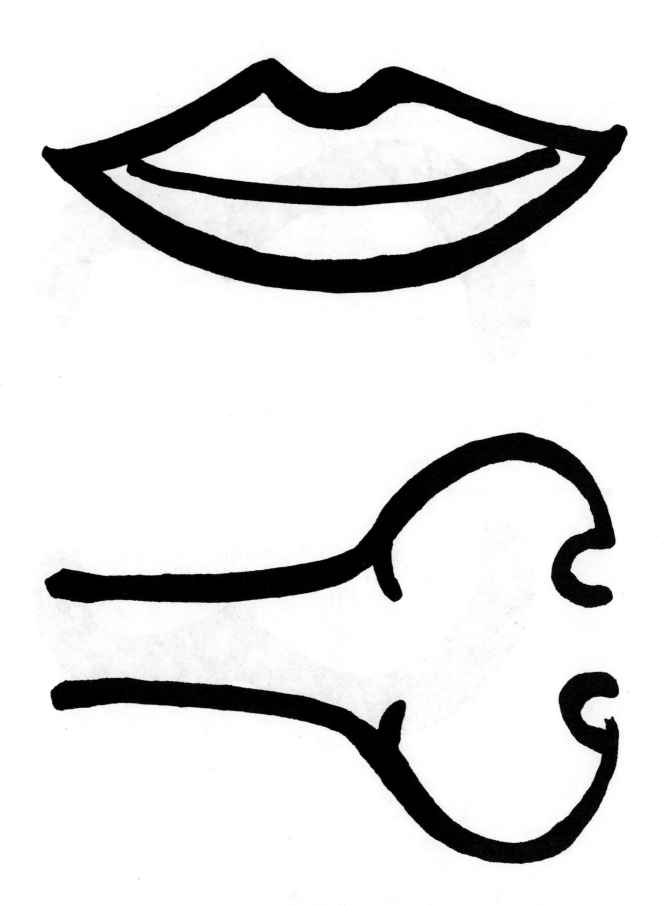

10a-182

10a-183

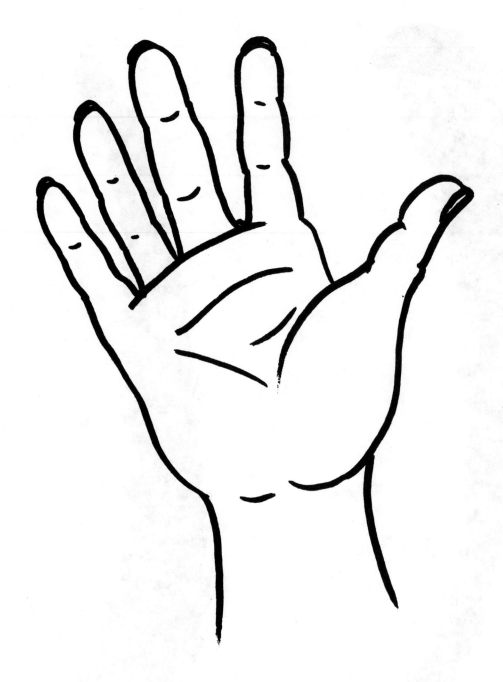

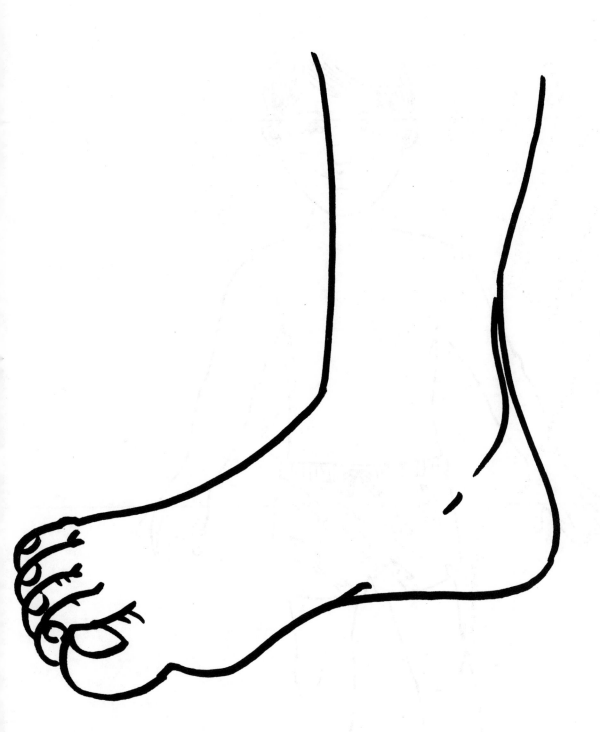

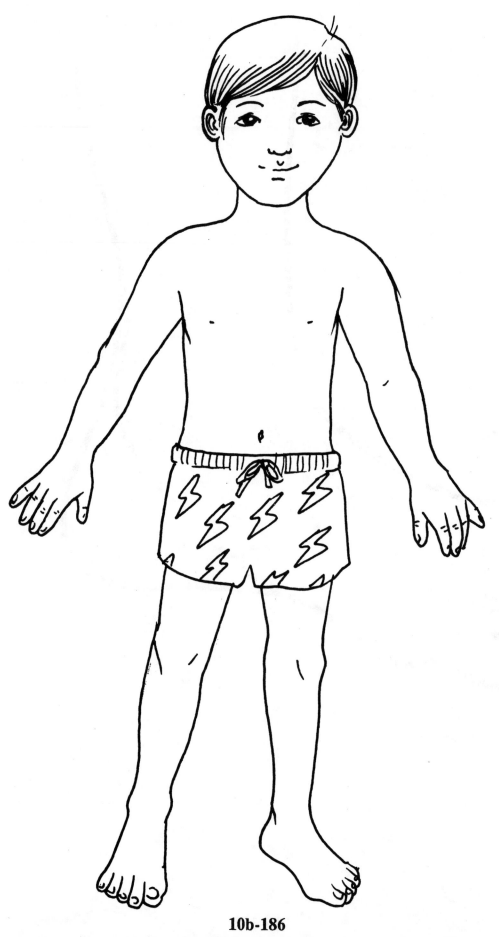

10b-186

APPENDIX B

SONGS

1. *SAYONARA*

Sayonara, sayonara   Goodbye, goodbye
Kore de kyoo wa   We must part and say goodbye
Owakare shimashoo   For today
Sayonara, sayonara   Goodbye, goodbye.

2. *AKAI TORI, KOTORI*

Akai tori, kotori   Red bird, little bird
Naze naze akai   Why oh why are you so red?
Akai mi o tabeta   Because I ate some red berries.

3. *GENKOTSU YAMA NO TANUKI-SAN*

Genkotsu yama no tanuki san   The little baby badger
Oppai nonde nenne shite   Drinks his milk and
Dakko shite onbu shite   takes a nap.
Mata ashita   I'll hold him and
JAN KEN PON   carry him on my back.
                              See you tomorrow!
                              JAN KEN PON

4. *ZOO-SAN*

Zoo-san, zoo-san   Mr. Elephant, Mr. Elephant
Ohana ga nagai no ne   Your nose is so long.
Soo yo, kaasan mo nagai no yo. Yes, my mother's is long, too.

5. KOTORI NO UTA

Kotori wa tottemo uta ga suki   The little bird loves to sing
Kaasan yobunomo uta de yobu   He calls his mother with a song
Pipipipipi chichichichichi   Pipipipipi chichichichichi
Pichikuripi   Pichikuripi

6. OHANASHI YUBI-SAN

Kono yubi otoosan futoocho otoosan
Ya a ya a ya a ya a wa ha ha ha ha ha ha
O hanashi   suru.

This is my father, my chubby father
Ya a ya a ya a ya a wa ha ha ha ha ha ha
He is talking to me.

7. TE O TATAKIMASHOO

Te o tatakimashoo   Let's clap our hands
Tan tan tan tan tan tan   tan tan tan tan tan tan
Ashibumi shimashoo   Let's stamp our feet
Tan tan tan tan tan tan   tan tan tan tan tan tan
Waraimashoo   Let's laugh out loud
A ha ha waraimashoo   a ha ha   let's laugh
A ha ha a ha ha a ha ha   a ha ha a ha ha a ha ha
Aa omoshiroi   Aa   isn't it fun.

8. MUSUNDE HIRAITE

Musunde hiraite   Make a fist, open it up
Te o utte musunde   Clap your hands and make a fist
Mata hiraite te o utte   Open it up and clap your hands
Sono te o ue ni   Put your hands up in the air
Musunde hiraite   Make a fist, open it up
Te o utte musunde   Clap your hands and make a fist.

188

9. *TULIPS*

Saita saita	All in bloom, all in bloom
Churippu no hana ga	The tulip blossoms are in bloom
Naranda naranda	All lined up, all lined up
Aka shiro kiiro	Red and white and yellow
Dono hana mitemo kirei da na.	Every flower that I see looks so pretty to me.

10. *OSHOGATSU*

Moo ikutsu neru to oshoogatsu	New Year's is coming soon
Oshoogatsu niwa tako agete	And we'll fly our kites
Koma o mawashite asobimashoo	We'll spin our tops and have lots of fun
Hayaku koi koi oshoogatsu	Hurry, hurry New Year's Day!

ZOO-SAN

Words: Michio Mado
Music: Ikuma Dan

Zoo san zoo san o ha na ga na ga i no ne

so yo ka a sa n mo na ga i no yo

OHANASHI YUBI-SAN

Words: Yoshiko Kooyama
Music: Akira Yuyama

ko no yu bi otoo san fu to o cho otoo san

ya a ya a ya a ya a wa ha ha ha ha ha ha

o ha na shi su ru

SAYONARA

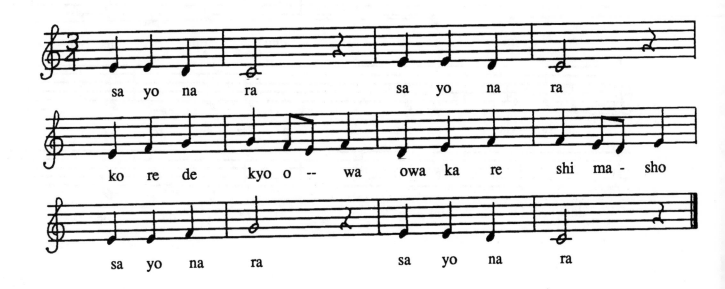

sa yo na ra　　　　sa yo na ra

ko re de kyo o -- wa owa ka re shi ma - sho

sa yo na ra　　　　sa yo na ra

GENKOTSUYAMA NO TANUKI-SAN

gen ko tsu ya ma no ta nu ki sa n

o ppa i no n de ne n ne shi te

da kko shi te on bu shi te ma ta a shi ta

TULIPS

Words: Takeshi Inoue
Music: Takeshi Inoue

sa i ta sa i ta chu ri ppu no ha na ga

na ran da na ran da a ka shi ro ki i ro

do no ha na mi te mo ki re i da na

OSHOOGATSU

Words: Kume Higashi
Music: Rentaro Taki

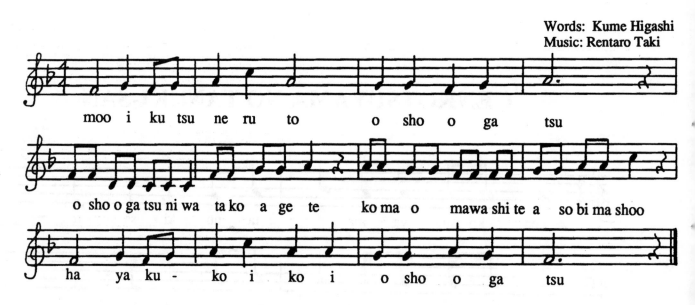

moo i ku tsu ne ru to o shoo ga tsu

o shoo ga tsu ni wa ta ko a ge te ko ma o mawa shi te a so bi ma shoo

ha ya ku - ko i ko i o shoo ga tsu

MUSUNDE HIRAITE

mu su n de hi ra i te te o u tte mu su n de

ma ta hi rai te te o u tte so no te o u e ni

mu su n de hi ra i te o u tte mu su n de

TE O TATAKIMASHOO

Words: Junichi Kobayashi

te o ta ta ki ma sho tan tan tan tan tan tan

a shi bu mi shi ma sho tan tan tan tan tan tan tan

wa rai ma sho a ha ha wa rai ma sho a ha ha

a ha ha a ha ha a a o mo shi ro i

AKAI TORI KOTORI

Words: Hakushu Kitahara
Music: Tamezo Narita

a kai to ri ko to ri

na ze na ze a ka i

a kai mi o ta be ta

KOTORI NO UTA

Words: Junichi Yoda
Music: Yasushi Akutagawa

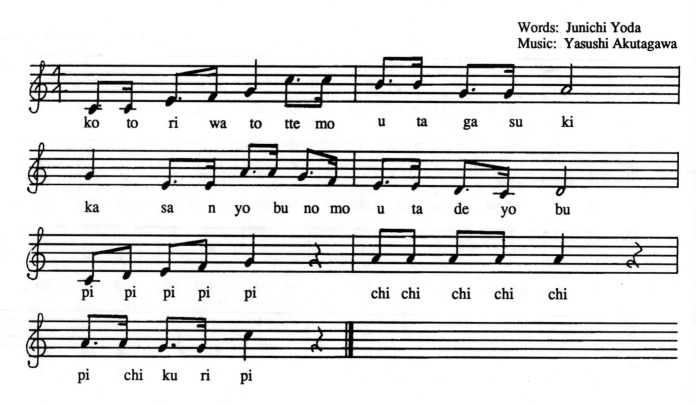

ko to ri wa to tte mo u ta ga su ki

ka sa n yo bu no mo u ta de yo bu

pi pi pi pi pi chi chi chi chi chi

pi chi ku ri pi